S0-ADE-791

THE CIRCLE OF FAITH

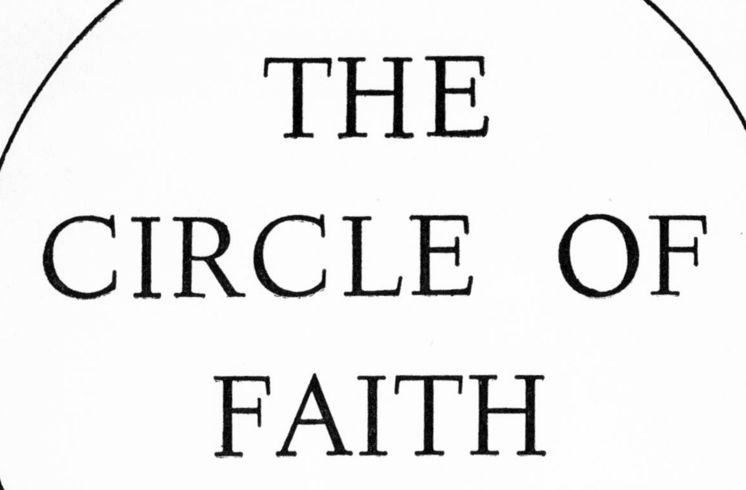

THE CIRCLE OF FAITH

by

MARCUS BACH

HAWTHORN BOOKS, INC.

Publishers

New York

This book was manufactured in the United States of America and published simultaneously in Canada by McClelland & Stewart, Ltd., 25 Hollinger Road, Toronto 16. Library of Congress Catalogue Card Number 57-6379.

FIRST EDITION
March, 1957

To

Pearl Warner

TABLE OF CONTENTS

1.

THE SEARCH

I once asked a priest to tell me the secret of the strength of Fulton Sheen. "That's easy," he replied. "It is all a matter of the disposition he has made of Jesus."

The answer had a familiar ring. It was identical with what a Methodist once told me about the power of "Big Bill" Stidger, Methodism's dramatic preacher, who drew thousands into his Kansas City church.

"The disposition he has made of Jesus" was evidently something that cut straight across denominational lines. It applied to Peter Marshall, a Presbyterian, who won the respect of official Washington as Senate Chaplain; it explained the success of John Haynes Holmes, a Unitarian, who built his Community Church in the heart of New York; it was the power behind the Lutheran liberal, Frank N. Buchman, who founded Moral Re-Armament; and it was the reason for the appeal of the Lutheran fundamentalist, Walter Meier, who started the "Lutheran Hour." It was the secret of success of Norman Vincent Peale, personalizer of religion for moderns, and also the reason for the achievement of Frank Laubach who brought spiritual light to many in jungle lands.

As I thought about it, it seemed to me that "the disposition he made of Jesus" was also the source of the spiritual strength of my old pastor uncle. The world never heard of him, but he catechized me in the fear of the Lord and, when I was fourteen, asked me point-blank what

I was going to do with Jesus. At the time I didn't quite know what he meant, but I knew that whatever he had done with Him, had made my uncle the most courageous and influential man in town.

Later I found this selfsame Jesus beckoning from the niches of many church walls and looking down from stained-glass windows all over the world. I heard about Him from Bible-banging evangelists shouting His words and from somber communicants who had taken Him into their hearts. I listened while He was discussed in classrooms and quoted in city parks and sacred groves. I heard Him prayed to in mansions and shacks, on country estates, and in the fields where crosses marked the graves of military dead.

Here was a Man who could not be avoided or put aside. He was always present—present in modern thought no less than in old theologies, present with men whether they used His name to curse or bless. Multitudes had to confess that whether they liked Him or not, He had to be reckoned with somewhere along the way.

I remember how, in my twenties, the Pentecostals bombarded me with a burning phrase, "Brother, have you received His baptism since you believed?" They had made a disposition of Him, too, and they told me it had made them "rich inside." It was always difficult for me to dodge their challenge when they asked me what I would some day do with Him.

During the years of my research which made me a participant in some forty religious movements, I discovered that believers in many denominations, cults, and sects all knew or claimed to know exactly what to do with this uncatchable Figure. These people never ceased to interest and intrigue me. Christian Scientists, Mormons, Jehovah's Witnesses, Adventists, well-known and little-known faiths, there were always those among them who knew what they believed about this Man. How sure they were of their opinions, how confident of themselves! How resolutely they walked with Him, hand in hand, as if He personally had called them from the Galilean lakeside with His "Follow me!"

In those days I wanted to believe that He had come into the world to unite the people, but the evidence was strong that He divided them. A great gulf separated Christian from non-Christian. There was a Scripture phrase which some had seized upon as though it were the hilt of the sword of truth: "There is no other name under heaven given among men, whereby we must be saved!" With this they cut a one-way path and, even though I felt it would not be quite like God to condemn those who had not accepted Him according to that view, I could find no argument with which to conquer theirs.

But if He separated Christian from non-Christian, He also separated Christian from Christian, dividing the members of the universal Christian family into nearly three hundred denominational children. When these religious varieties were sifted down, it was apparent that an interpretation of Him or an opinion about Him was often the sole reason for schism and strife. One group insisted He was this and another claimed He was that.

One would say, "He came to found a church."

"Why, no," another would reply. "He never had that in mind."

"He wants His followers to have no fellowship with the world."

"Why, not at all. He ate with sinners."

"He wants to be worshiped as Lord and King."

"Oh, surely not! He plainly said He didn't want that!"

"He was perfect and we ought also to be perfect if we claim to follow Him."

"How can that be? He said that there was no one good but God."

And that was why my hobby of inquiring into what people believe developed into a profession. I felt that the sum total of what men professed about this controversial Messiah would constitute the most valid Christian faith that anyone could find. And how was I to discover what people believed about Him if I did not meet all the people? One encounter with a believer was always worth a hundred books; one interview was better than a thousand secondhand reports. Surely the mystery about Him would be solved if I searched out those who had made Him the pivotal factor in their lives.

"What do you think of Jesus?" I asked Kagawa, the Japanese evangelist who, though nearly blind, was still urged on to learn of Him.

"He is a Light that shines in men's souls," Kagawa said. "He is strength for the weak and living sight for the blind."

"What do you think of Jesus?" I put the question to Frank B. Robinson, founder of Psychiana and a religious revolutionary, as I rode with him in his Cadillac.

"A great man," he snapped back. "A revolutionary. If He were living today he'd go about his preaching driving a Cadillac and wearing a Stetson hat."

"What do you think of Jesus?" I inquired of a Trappist monk.

He placed his finger to his lips. Even though he had permission to speak, he would give me no answer. Surely I already knew that Jesus would be like the Trappist, secluded from the world, a celibate, a religious contemplative, obedient, poor, loving heaven more than the world, and pledged to perpetual silence.

In Chichicastenango, a lame boy offered to guide me into the hills for a service of the Quiche-Mayas.

"What do you think of Jesus?" I ventured.

"My Jesus," he said, "He helps me walk."

There He was, this controversial Figure, sight for the blind, a revolutionary for a revolutionist, silence for the silent one, legs for the lame.

On the creosoted wall of a German refugee shack I saw a battered crucifix. The prematurely old woman followed my gaze. "We found it on a battlefield," she explained. "It is a comfort. If we did not have Jesus—what then?"

Yes, they told me that. "If we did not have Jesus, what then?" High churchmen and low, worshipers in cathedrals and at camp meetings, followers of old faiths and new, revivalists, radio preachers, TV healers—all boasted that they had made their disposition of this imponderable Man.

Sometimes a telltale sign gave me an answer. In a Chicago office I saw an affirmation card fixed prominently above the executive's desk. It read, "Against the measure of His code, I find the guide for my conduct. Against the goodness of His Acts, I weigh my motives. Against the greatness of His faith, I test my charity."

While I was asking others what they thought of Him, others were asking me. What was *my* answer? When would I learn to read aright the many dimensions of this Sojourner who was found anew by every generation, in every place, and through every new and changing thought? Could any individual or any group be totally right about Him and all others wholly wrong? If everyone was right, where were the heretics? If all were wrong, then where was Truth?

So I set out on what developed into a forty-thousand-mile quest to visit certain persons who for many years had tantalized my thinking. Their lives and their discoveries had hinted that they had fully come to terms with this Man from Nazareth and the public and the press always seemed to agree.

Who were these people? Among them: a peasant woman in a German village not far from the Iron Curtain; a Persian author in Haifa under the guarding shadow of Mt. Carmel; an immortal, world-traveling American; a high church dignitary in the Eternal City; a doctor in an African jungle. These were my primary sources, and it is from them I take courage to write of their relationship —and mine—to Him.

2.

THERESE NEUMANN

1.

First of all there was Therese.

I had heard about her long years ago, on a Sunday afternoon in the spring of 1927, to be exact. I remember how my dad looked up from his newspaper and called to my mother in the kitchen, "Here's something you'll be interested in."

While Mother stood in the room, industriously wiping a platter, Dad read a story that had come out of Germany. It told about a Bavarian girl who on Good Friday had bled in hands and feet, a sympathetic sufferer with Jesus on the Cross. Furthermore, it was claimed that this remarkable Fräulein had embarked on a perpetual fast, eating nothing now but a small wafer every day.

My mother was intensely interested in religion, but on hearing this account she gave the platter an impatient swish.

"Such craziness!" she exclaimed. "That sounds to me like a swindle."

Dad took a thoughtful drag on his cigar, blew a puff of smoke toward heaven and, with a sly wink at me, commented, "Swindle? Maybe it's a miracle." He always took as easy a view of religion as he did of life.

I lived back through this Sunday memory recently when cabman Michael Mehler of Marktredwitz drove me to Therese's hometown, Konnersreuth, near the Czech border. Herr Mehler said he had never driven over icier roads, but he liked to try the impossible.

Incidentally, he was a philosopher. A participant in two wars, wounded, but still very much alive, he had his creed: the best preacher is a man's conscience; the best teacher is time; the best book is experience; and the best business is driving a cab.

Though risking the loss of a fare, he said to me, "I've taken better people than you over here and they didn't get to see Therese. I don't know why you think you can do it." He didn't know that I, too, like to try the impossible.

Musing on his words, I envisioned the parade that had passed Therese Neumann's door during the past quarter century. Doctors, churchmen, magicians, government officials, newsmen, spiritualists, Christians, Jews, Moslems, Buddhists and Hindu swamis—all had been pilgrims on this rambling road to Konnersreuth.

I asked Herr Mehler, "What do you think of Therese? Does she really have the marks of the nails and do her hands and feet actually bleed during Holy Week?"

"Of course."

"Are you personally acquainted with her?"

"I often see her. She comes to Marktredwitz every now and then. She is just like anybody else. Only she's more religious."

"Do you believe she hasn't eaten anything for over twenty years, nothing but the wafer every day?"

He shrugged. "If God wants it that way, why can't He have it that way?"

On this Sunday afternoon, Konnersreuth looked like a Currier & Ives print: the little houses clustering around the church, children on sleighs, an old man pulling a child on a sled, a housewife lugging an armful of wood with her apron tucked up over it—these set the mood for a crisp and crackling Sabbath day.

Herr Mehler got the cab up the slippery incline to the house after several tries. This far he had promised to take me; now it was up to me. He said he would wait.

I rapped at the cold door which bore a typed note stating that whoever wished to see Therese Neumann would have to get permission from the priest.

An elderly woman let me in. She was a bit annoyed that anyone should come at such an inopportune time, two-thirty on the day for rest, but I was cold and she took pity on me. She led me into a small, cozy room where a fire burned. She said she would summon the priest.

The room was like the town; intimate. The crucifix on the plain wall, the picture of the Sacred Heart with brittle palm branches stuck behind it, and a rosary dangling from the picture's frame united Rome with Konnersreuth. A glassed-in bookcase served as a shrine for a few reliquaries and also for a packet wrapped in cloth as though it were precious.

Father Joseph Naber came quietly into the room, glanced at me, then, turning his back, closed the door. In appearance and action he fitted perfectly into this setting. He was eighty-two, stooped with what seemed more to be humility than age, and his eyes looked at me quizzically through thick-lensed spectacles. He extended a hand.

"You come on such a day!" he said in mild astonishment. "Over this ice and snow? Children are skating in the streets."

He was more impressed that I had come over the slippery road from Marktredwitz than that I had made the trip from America.

"So you want to see our Resl," he murmured with a sigh that said no one ever came for any other purpose. "Everyone wants to see our Resl. Why?"

It was a good question. I could have said, "Curiosity," and that would have been true. I could have told him I wanted to do a story about her, on the purported bleeding, the stigmata, so called, and the incredible legend that here was a woman who lived without food. That, too, would have been true. I told him I was interested in people who had found something to live by, and that was also true. That pleased him and he said he would send Therese in. Was it, I wondered, to be as easy as this?

Something to live by. The impact of this provocative phrase deepened in the stillness of the room. Some people had all the answers. I didn't, but here in Konnersreuth I told myself again that even though a man might never find his way to the top of the religious mountain, he need not stay in the valley.

I looked out through the window. Herr Mehler sat in the car, coat pulled up under his chin, puffing at a cigarette. He had told me that even though he ran the finest cab in town, he kept his rates low so the average man could afford them. I had neglected to ask him how much he charged for waiting.

2.

I turned quickly at the sound of the opening door. A woman stood with her hand on the knob. She was buxom and strong, with a round, rosy face and mellow eyes. A white headscarf tied under her chin with the flourish of a bow contrasted strikingly with the styleless black dress. I looked at her and a thought flashed through my mind: If you're Therese, you've been lunching somewhere along the way!

Our eyes met. She was smiling. She seemed to say, Well, what did you expect to see? A ghost or a shadow? What strange ideas people have!

She closed the door, pressed her fingers to her cheeks and said, "My face! I think it must be frozen."

As she did this, I saw on the back of each hand a bloody scar.

So this was Therese. This very human, easy-to-talk-to, gentle and good-humored peasant woman of fifty-six was the one around whom stories of mystery and magic, miracle and fraud, had been woven. This was the world's greatest stigmatist or the perpetrator of the world's greatest hoax. Either she had tapped some hidden power, or she held the secret formula for grand deception.

Yes, this was Therese and her first remark had suggested that she was not immune to pain. This was she whom Father Naber had described in a phrase, "*Unser*

Resl ist ein einfaches Mädel. (Our Resl is a guileless maiden.)"

Her manner was shy yet forceful, despite its bafflling combination of courtesy and caution. Her friendly invitation in German, "Come, then, sit down. Here there is no formality," put me at ease, though it made me wonder again what right I had to dabble in her faith when I had difficulty in understanding my own. But here was Therese, expressing genuine interest in me and my visit. It was as though I bore knowledge of another way of life, a way not exactly holy, but one that could be conquered at any moment by her combative self-assurance.

She poked up the fire, then seated herself opposite me, resting her scarred hands on the table beneath the crucifix.

"So, now," she said with a smile, "here we are."

"So, now," I replied, adopting her friendly mood, "tell me about Therese Neumann."

"Only because you have come so far," she warned. "For, believe me, I have no interest in having you write my life story."

"Many are interested in you," I reminded her.

She sighed.

"They shouldn't be." Her gaze was suddenly faraway. "They should be interested only in One. Yes, yes, that One."

Her expression left no doubt about Whom she had in mind. Her eyes, unaware of me to whom so much of worldly things still clung, rested lingeringly on the crucifix.

It was a long moment before her attention again turned to me. Her story began with her girlhood's ambition to be a "mission sister" in Africa. The oldest of eleven children, she knew something about service to others. Her family was poor. Her father, the town tailor, had also tried his hand at farming, and Therese often "worked like a man" in the fields. Nothing about the hardship of a mission assignment could frighten her. She always felt that the more difficult the task the more valuable the training in fulfilling the call from God.

World War I opened her teen-age eyes to the cruelties of which men are capable. The death and destruction around her painted a new and terrifying picture of the world; got in the way of her worship and prayer; filled her with questions. She wondered how it was possible for the children of God to become so easily the servants of evil? Had it always been this way, even in the days when the Son of God walked the earth as the Incarnation of Love? Men had rejected Him then, and now was He again being denied by those who should honor Him? Was her Jesus once more being led to the Cross?

Then came the accident. A fire alarm brought the people to a burning home whose flames endangered the whole village of Konnersreuth. Frantic citizens formed a bucket brigade. Therese, a link in the chain of volunteers, stood on a chair and passed pails of water to a man on a ladder. The flaming heat, with the frenzied shouting for greater speed, made her hysterical. Suddenly her arms stiffened and, reeling, she fell headlong to the ground.

They carried her to her home where, for days and weeks, she suffered from shock and head wounds.

"After that I was in the hospital many times," she explained, as she relived the events. "I could never stand for long without a sense of falling. My head was always aching inside and out. I was told that nothing could be done for me. I would come home and try to work, but I was so unsteady that I had to hold on to something. Once I fell down the cellar stairs. Another time I fell from a ladder and was unconscious. Soon afterwards I began to lose my sight. I felt that now it would mean darkness for the rest of my life. I wondered what would become of me. I wondered about God. I thought, 'Why did He put the idea that I should be a missionary in my heart if He does not want me to go?' From 1918 on, even though I often tried to work, I had to lie in bed most of the time."

As if suddenly realizing that what she was saying was being jotted down, she broke off abruptly.

"Why do you want to know all this?"

"You are one of the mysterious people in the world. The mark of the nails . . ."

"Yes, that," she said and looked at her hands as if the wounds were a source of perpetual comfort as well as concern. A knowing smile crossed her face. Then she related how the philosophy of suffering came to her. One day on her sick bed she heard of a student for the priesthood who had to leave the seminary because of a throat ailment.

"I said to myself," she confided, " 'Why doesn't God

give me that sickness, whatever it is? With all that I suffer already, one more ache or pain won't make any difference! I will take the young man's disease upon myself. Wasn't there One who carried our burdens, and does He perhaps want me to do the same?' "

So she began to pray for the power to suffer vicariously for the student. Gradually her throat became affected. Day by day she found it more difficult to speak. After that her throat was continually sore. And while all this was happening the young seminarian in a distant village felt himself getting well and soon returned to school.

This was the beginning of Therese's burden-bearing, and it became one of the disputed wonders of Konnersreuth. She healed her father of rheumatism by taking it upon herself. She cured the stomach ailment of a farm woman by saying that out of compassion she would endure that, too. A hospital patient's fever left when it was "transferred to Therese." A soldier "gave her" the infection of a wound that he might live. Mothers, it was reported, let her bear the pain of childbirth. The lame hobbled to Konnersreuth and many left their crutches and canes at the Neumann home. The blind came, too, and often, it was claimed, their sight was restored. Seriously, but also in jest, a saying went around among the sick and near-sick of the region, "Give it to Therese!"

During the years 1918 to 1922, in which she was the willing recipient of others' aches and pains, Therese was blind, partially paralyzed, and often at the point of death. Doctors disagreed in their opinions. Some said she was an exhibitionist, a neurotic, a religious fanatic.

A story was retold, and freely admitted by Therese, that, shortly before the accident which started her on her career of sickness, she was criminally attacked one night on a country road. She beat off her assailant, ran home, locked herself in her room and spent hours in prayer. "Fixed in her mind," said a physician, "was the deep-seated belief that sex, as well as war, made beasts of men. From this time on her affection turned completely to Jesus, who, alone among men, was perfect and pure."

Most of the villagers, however, maintained that her sickness was organic, and these also had their supporters in the medical profession. On April 28, 1923, a physician prescribed a new "wonder drug" to cure Therese's blindness.

The drug was never used. Before her father could get it from the city, Resl's sight "miraculously" returned.

"It came back to me like a wonderful light," she told me. "That was April 29, the day on which Pope Pius XI made Therese of Lisieux a saint. You know about Therese of Lisieux? She knew what it is to love Jesus. When she was dying and was asked what she was saying in her prayers, she said, 'Nothing. I love Him.' "

"Was Therese of Lisieux a special favorite of yours?" I asked.

"Of course. My namesake."

"You thought about her a great deal? And read about her? And wanted to be like her?"

"That is not a bad wish, is it?"

"So when she was canonized——?"

"My sight came back."

"All at once?"

"Yes, that is the way it was. Darkness dropped away and I could see."

"At the very moment of the canonization?"

"I think it must have been. Yes, I think someone has checked that. My goodness, everything that has ever happened to me has been checked, you know!"

"Then what happened?"

"One of my sisters went to tell Father Naber. He came running over and said, 'Tell me, Resl, how it was. How did it happen?' "

"What did you say?"

"What could I say? Only that I had a vision."

"You saw someone in this vision?"

"Of course. It was the Holy Maria."

"Did you hear a voice?"

"Yes."

"What did it say?"

"It said, 'You have taken the sickness of others and have patiently carried your own. The Blessed Master wills that you should see.' Then, when I thanked the vision, it said, 'Therese, would you not also like to walk again?' "

"What did you say to that?"

"I said, 'To walk or not to walk—to lie here or not to lie here—it doesn't matter. Whatever He wants me to do, that is good enough for me.' "

In her next vision she saw Jesus and at the recollection of this she clasped her hands in ecstasy.

"What shall I say?" she demanded. "Soon I was sitting

on the side of the bed. I knew I would walk again. But all that is only physical. Think of what happened in my heart! I saw Him! I heard Him speak! What more does a person want than that? What more is there to live for than that?"

"Then crowds really did start coming to Konnersreuth?" I prompted.

"Oh, yes. My goodness, such crowds!" Therese confronted me with great earnestness. "How do you explain it? Why should people want to make a spectacle of these things? That is not the idea. That is not what Jesus wants. Who am *I* that anyone should come to see me?"

Once more I had to say, "You are an attraction."

"Like a doll or a puppet?" she countered, with a hearty laugh. "No, please believe me, I do not want any publicity. I do not want to be an attraction. All I want," she said in a whisper, "is to be with Him." Then, clasping her hands over her breast, she exclaimed, "Why do you think He chose me?"

"Maybe because you chose Him."

Her eyes hovered over me. Then her gaze drifted off into space. It was as though she saw someone or something that I did not see. For her the colorless wall must have opened or perhaps the crucifix came to life. She extended her arms as though to give herself over to the Man on the Cross. The flicker of a smile played at her lips. Her eyes closed. She seemed to stop breathing. She sat like a medium in a trance. It could easily have been an act; but it might well have been the deepest possible moment of religious awareness.

She sat this way, oblivious of me, impervious to the world around her, for perhaps five minutes. A few times her lips moved. I expected her to speak, but the silence in the room only deepened. Hypnotized, she sat there. Then she slowly lowered her arms, opened her eyes, sighed heavily and asked, "Now, what were you saying?"

"You chose Him," I repeated.

There was a faraway look in her eyes.

"He is wonderful," she said softly.

"Therese," I asked, "may I examine your hands?"

"Of course!"

The wound in each was deep. It was as though long ago a nail had been driven through the palm. The scars were a transparent film of skin covering small dark wells of blood.

When these first appeared, in the spring of 1926, a few weeks before Easter, Therese, as always, was thinking of Jesus.

There, in the long-ago quietness of her room, with the afternoon light waning, she visualized Him in Gethsemane. How much He had to endure! How greatly had He suffered! How often must He have asked, "Why, O God, must I endure all this?" Surely by now He must have seen the Cross! He must already have felt the nails in His hands and the sharp cut of the spear in his side as He knelt there upon the great rock!

As Therese dwelt on this she had become aware of a pain in her left side, just beneath her heart. She put her hand to the spot, then drew it back, the fingers red with blood. "This," she thought, "is a sign of my approaching death. I am pierced as He was and I shall go to Him."

The bleeding continued for several hours. She told no one about it except her sister-in-law who was caring for her at the time. She lay with closed eyes waiting for death. Moments passed. Strangely, she felt no weaker. Further, the pain in her head and the throbbing in her ears had disappeared.

"I was thinking only of Him," was her explanation, "and that leaves no time for thought of self."

Then came Holy Week, the week of Christ's passion. Therese, knowing every detail of those holy days, followed "her Jesus" through each scene of His betrayal. As though she herself were living it, she pictured His arrest, His trial, His condemnation. When He was turned over to the mob in bonds, she felt that she, too, was thrown mercilessly upon the world. When He began His march to Calvary, she felt the weight of the Cross. Whenever He paused to gather strength, she was with Him. When He was whipped, she felt the pain. His agony was hers and finally, there on Golgotha, the nails were also driven through her hands and feet.

3.

So it was that on Good Friday in 1926 the stigmata appeared, first in the right hand and then in the left; and when asked if she herself had inflicted these wounds, she could only shake her head and say, "No. It is His passion." Those who witnessed that first manifestation said that she seemed almost to have suffered death with Him.

The wounds remained open for two weeks. Then a new skin began to form, covering the sores with a thin tissue. On many Fridays throughout the years the scars would open and bleed; and, on each Good Friday, they were accompanied by the marks of the nails in the feet, an occasional bleeding in the wounded side and, several times, by the mark of the thorns on Therese's head. Tears and blood usually streamed from her eyes just before the final agony.

As I sat with this mysterious woman in the inner world of her experience, I seemed to hear my mother say, "It sounds like a swindle." And I heard my father's thoughtful remark, "Maybe a miracle."

Among the thousands who sought the answer, whose faith or the lack of it drew them to Konnersreuth, were doctors and psychologists who tried to measure the relationship between human capacity for suffering and human love for the divine. Before their science could solve this mystery, however, an even greater one was posed for them: Therese "gave up eating."

After the stigmata appeared in 1926, she drank only a small cup of tea daily. This was reduced to a spoonful. Then even this was rejected in favor of one daily morsel, the Blessed Sacrament, a small unleavened wafer, followed by a sip of water. In 1927 rumor spread that she had given up the water, too, and that only the wafer now passed her lips.

The credulous believed it. The holy wished it to be true. To these few, it was a miracle; to the many, it was "just another swindle."

But how true was it?

Therese had been fasting for a year when the Church sent three nurses, under a doctor's supervision, to keep her under strict surveillance for a two-week period. There was never a moment during this time that the Maid of Konnersreuth was not carefully watched. She could not have taken a crumb of bread without detection and yet, for fourteen days, she went about her work as usual, eating only the daily wafer.

Weighed at regular periods, it was noted that she lost three pounds during her "passion with the Lord"—the day the stigmata appeared—and then regained this weight almost immediately. Her temperature fluctuated with her suffering. Blood, saliva, and other tests showed no unusual results. Guarded in her sleep as well as during her waking hours, she was checked for signs of hysteria and tested as to her desire for food. It was reported that she was always "normal," with the exception that "she does not want to eat." The conclusions, issued under the *Bischöfliche Ordinariat Regensburg,* declared that Therese drank nothing, ate only the Sacrament for two full weeks, and showed no ill effects.

To my laconic question, "How does it feel not to eat?" she promptly replied, "How is it to eat?" and her good-natured laughter indicated that at this point we were worlds apart.

"Therese, do you remember a Dr. Buchinger?"

"So many doctors have been here," she lamented with a sigh, as though she hoped I would not again bring in someone to find out whether or not she ever raided the pantry shelves.

"He was here years ago," I explained, "and brought another medical doctor with him. Also a philosopher and a biologist."

"Learned men," she affirmed with a nod, but she was not inquisitive. She asked me nothing more about them.

I had heard of Dr. Otto Buchinger through his son, Hans, a graduate student in one of my university classes. Hans related how his father, skeptical of the reports coming out of Konnersreuth, had decided to investigate. Prior to his visit, he had already dismissed the matter of stigmatism as a "psycho-physical reaction" and, in his private judgment, considered the talk of a prolonged fast as "pure fable."

One thing bothered him, however. He had asked a well-known criminologist of Leipzig whether it would be possible for anyone to deceive investigators, examiners, the Church, and the inquisitive public, especially neighbors and friends, throughout a ten-year period without ever being exposed or discredited. The criminologist flatly asserted that this was beyond the realm of probability. "What, then, in heaven's name, is going on at Konnersreuth?" asked Dr. Buchinger.

He came with his colleagues to the village of mystery and, after a thorough clinical study of Therese, published an answer to his own question in a pamphlet *Wirkliches und Wirkendes (The Real and the Workable).*

"I must declare," wrote this noted German specialist,

"that, despite all care and watchfulness, we were unable to arrive at any conclusion or explanation as to the fasting of Therese Neumann, or as to the phenomena of the stigmata. There is no indication that hysteria is here at work. What can we conclude but that in the truly devout Stigmatist of Konnersreuth there is—whether we like it or not—something spiritual which causes these phenomena. All honor to our science and its methods, but here something is at work which defies rational explanation. So it seems to me. In this case, we must evidently leave the solid ground of our science and enter the realm of parapsychology, mystery, and magic which, today, is more than speculation and belief and is, rather, the opening door to a certain state of empirical knowledge."

Student Hans Buchinger, also, had seen and remembered Therese.

"She sat with her back to the light," he once told me, "and under her dark head covering I saw a pallid face. It was not the bloodless appearance of a sick person, but rather that of an ascetic with eyes from which rays appeared to stream. She spoke about the Sacrament with the faith and enthusiasm of a child who tells about something she deeply loves. I saw in her hands the mark of the stigmata. She made such an impression upon me that my suspicions, like my father's, left me. Today I often think of her and feel that the idea of The Holy which emanated from her has for me linked the temporal with the eternal."

Therese would only say of the Buchingers, "They must

be good people. But all people are good. They come and go. What is one to say?"

She meant, "What is one to say about the things that happen to me? Am I not just an ordinary woman, an '*einfaches Mädel*'?"

Then she sighed.

"They tell me, Therese," I probed, "that you are clairvoyant."

She wanted an explanation, reminding me with a smile that "big words" were not for her. If I meant her ability to foretell events before they happened or to "see things" which others did not see, what answer could she make to that? Sometimes, in moments of great affection for Him, she was lost to the present world. In what she said and did then, she was only the instrument of a higher power.

"Is it true that you can read sealed messages?"

"Oh," she said, "so they say."

"Is it true that Hitler was so impressed with your abilities that he said you should not be molested?"

"I was not mistreated," she replied.

"Some say you were treated well by the Third Reich because you have a great following. Others tell me that their interest had to do with your psychical powers."

She leaned imploringly across the table.

"You see," she said, "that is why these interviews are so difficult. People want me to say things that I myself do not understand or know very much about. They want to make an attraction of me, and that is just what I do not want."

She leaned back and dropped her hands in her lap.

"One more question," I urged. "It is said that you speak Aramaic, though you have never studied languages. . ."

"That is another one of those same things," she interrupted. "These things all happen when I am with Him."

She was relieved that Father Naber came into the room at this moment. It must have been an answer to her wish. A glance passed between them. She got up and went out almost at once.

4.

"Well," said the priest genially, "you had a good visit? Did you get all the information you wanted?"

"There are still unanswered questions, Father," I told him, leafing through my notes.

"Those there will always be," he reflected with a smile.

"You have been with Therese ever since these strange happenings began," I reminded him. "Tell me, what do you honestly think of all this?"

He lifted a hand as if to say, "Wait and I will tell you." Then he took from the bookcase the little packet of cloth. He laid this on the table and unfolded it reverently.

"I do not show this to everyone who comes here," he said. "This jacket is what Resl wore once when the wound appeared in her side. See the stain of blood? This kerchief I myself placed on her head during one of her moments of suffering. See, here are small marks of blood as though they might have been made by a crown of thorns. And this blouse became bloodstained when it was worn during a time of Therese's great agony in Passion Week."

"Do the stigmata appear every year during that week?"

"Not always. I think the reason may be that so many people come only out of curiosity, with no spiritual thoughts in mind. God is not interested in showing signs and wonders just to satisfy the doubting."

"But isn't that a good reason for these manifestations —to convince the skeptics?"

"There is but one reason," he said. "God's will. And why God chose Therese Neumann for this, or why He chooses another for something else, are things beyond our knowing."

He was tying the white ribbon around these mysterious memorabilia when the door opened. Therese had returned.

"A gift for you," she said proudly, "a remembrance for you of your visit."

She put two small lithographed cards into my hands. One was a copy of Dürer's *Infant Jesus;* the other, a print of Rothenburg's *Head of Christ,* wearing the crown of thorns. On the back of each card she had written, "His love go with you. Therese Neumann."

"But now," she said with sudden concern, "I must go or the whole Sunday will have slipped away from me."

"Yes, yes," agreed Father Naber and, as I expressed my thanks, Therese returned to her duties as housekeeper in Father Naber's home, and friend to all who required her help.

"Well," said the priest after she had gone, "now you have seen our Resl and now you have something by which to remember her."

"Tell me," I said, "those reports of Therese's prolonged fast . . . Is it true that she has eaten nothing since 1926?"

His answer was prompt and emphatic. "I tell you on my honor as a priest, and before the sight of God, she has eaten nothing except the Blessed Sacrament."

"Do you expect the Church to make an official statement on these happenings here at Konnersreuth?"

"Ah, that," he said, "what can I say? Mother Church makes up her mind slowly in these matters. She must be unquestionably sure on every detail."

"But as for you?" I prodded.

"I already know," was his pronouncement.

He went with me to the door and spoke a greeting to my cabman who was walking around in an effort to keep warm. Then he watched us silently as we started down the icy slope that led back to the Marktredwitz road.

"So," Herr Mehler complained, "first I wondered whether you were going to get in and then I began to wonder whether you would ever come out."

"I'll make it right with you."

"You Americans! You make everything right with money! I don't care about your money. What did you find out about Resl?"

" '*An einfaches Mädel*'," I told him.

"Oh, no," he said, "that isn't enough. Tell me what you found out. Why do you think you can always ferret ideas out of others and never express your own? Come, now, what do *you* think?"

Herr Mehler was unflatteringly right. For many years I had been prying into people's beliefs without committing myself on my own. My aim was to do a reporter's job. I wished to be an observer only. I took religion the way my dad had taken it, "easy like." Yet my statement to Father Naber was true. I *was* looking for something, and what had I learned from Therese? What did I think of her? Were her experiences in the line of miracles or just plain swindles?

"Well, Herr Mehler," I said, "some day when I come to a conclusion I'll write and tell you."

He grunted in distaste and readied himself for conquering the icy road ahead.

5.

Months have passed since I paid this cabman his very moderate fee, and the time is overdue for me to send the promised letter to him. For I have arrived at an opinion about Therese Neumann and it is one which I am eager to share. It will, I am sure, be of interest to Herr Mehler. It may even help other cabmen and other pilgrims who venture over good roads, and bad, on their spiritual quest.

I found the answer to "our Resl" neither in Marktredwitz nor in Konnersreuth, but in Jerusalem. In Bethany, to be exact, where I walked the streets where Jesus walked. Very likely these are not the same streets, for stones have been put upon stones since His day and this Holy City has changed hands at least twenty times since He lived there among His people. But as I tramped the dusty, walled-in thoroughfares, I said what every other pilgrim has surely said or thought or felt, "Perhaps it was here that Jesus set His feet."

I thought of Therese when I visited the partially restored home of Martha and Mary. The original house must have been little more than a cave. The "porch" where Jesus sat with Mary was the dust of the road. The kitchen where Martha rattled the pots and pans was only a cubicle.

But Therese came to mind here. She was Mary and she loved Him. She sat with Him, lost in His presence and attentive to His words. Therese also came to mind when I was shown the station of the Cross where Veronica gave the suffering Jesus a kerchief with which to wipe His face. I thought of her when I stood alone in the room where Mary Magdalene washed His feet, and where the cruse of precious ointment was broken. I thought of her when I stood on Golgotha where Mary the Mother saw Him die.

It seemed to me miraculous that out of settings such as these, out of surroundings so primitive, so abject, there came a Man with a philosophy so great that we, with all our progress, wisdom, and skill, have never quite been able to meet His challenge or live His words.

And it occurred to me again that, since He came into the world with such startling force, since He so changed the thought and culture of His time and ours, *no one* could possibly escape the need for making some disposition of Him. There He walked, and we were bound to meet Him. There He sat, and we could not help but catch some of the words He spoke. There He lived, and it was inevitable that we all should brush shoulders with Him.

This helped me to understand Therese. There was a time in her life when her path crossed the path of the Man from Nazareth. Like every other thoughtful person she made a decision about Him. It might not have been my decision or Herr Mehler's decision or the decision of many others. God, loving variety, made us all different, even in our religious attitudes.

Let it suffice that Therese's path crossed His and when it did she began to love Him as a lover loves. He came to her on the level of her desires, on the level of the highest thought of which she was capable. Was it good or bad, right or wrong, miracle or swindle? That is beside the point. It was simply the result of one individual's meeting with the Man. There is that type of mind—Therese's type. When it meets Him, it makes of Him a Sentiment and an Emotion.

Had Therese lived when Jesus lived, she would have been exactly the kind of person Mary was. Martha, working in the kitchen, would have evoked from her only a sigh: "Who can think about food at a time like this?" Like Mary, she would have been fascinated and enthralled by His presence. Like Mary Magdalene she, too, would have washed His feet and dried them with her hair. Like Veronica she would have given Him her kerchief with which to wipe the sweat from His cheeks on the way to Calvary. Like Mary the Mother, she would have been the last to forsake Him on the Cross.

Therese met Him face to face in Konnersreuth and, for her, life was never the same again. This encounter changed her world. Religion had linked her to Rome; Jesus united her with Jerusalem. He became her heart's desire, her Sentiment and her Emotion.

I have no doubt that some day science will establish her agony of Holy Week as sympathetic suffering endured because of her all-surpassing love for Him. No one who has seen her can doubt that "feasting on His presence" is to her as nourishing and as satisfying as food. She needs no intellectual warranty of His greatness, no proof that He is philosophically without peer, no scholasticism to put Him at the top of her list of those upon whom the thought of the world must rely. She loves Him and for her there is no more mature decision to be made.

Does she know what He had in mind for the plan of salvation? It is love. Does she have an answer to the why of service or the when of decision? Love is the answer. Does she question the nature of church organization, the rise of dogmas, the demand of creed? It is love.

Blithely, irrevocably, almost despiteful of the fretful search by any other road than that of love, she believes that He lived and loved and died for her. She takes all the logic-chopping, head-splitting argumentation about Him, and all the theological potpourri which has built new faiths and perpetuated old ones, which has destroyed empires and beheaded kings, and throws the whole terrible mess overboard to be sunk in the sea of love.

To the exasperation of many and the delight of others, to the consternation of some and the amazement of all, she openly and publicly claims Him for her personal affection. She is desperately, deeply, violently in love with Him.

There is that type of mind—Therese's type.

3.

SHOGHI EFFENDI

1.

There was also Shoghi Effendi.

A cable addressed to me at Geneva and forwarded to me in the Holy Land, said, "Shoghi Effendi will see you. Advise him time of your arrival."

He was in the north, in Haifa, Israel. I was in the south, in Jerusalem, Jordan. Between us was the Mandelbaum Gate, the only corridor between Arab countries and Israel and it was open, as far as Jordan was concerned, to one-way passage exclusively. "If a traveler goes to Israel, let him stay there or go on his way to a neutral country." This was Jordanian policy and there were few exceptions. Mine was one.

When I walked through the Gate, that barren 300-foot stretch of No Man's Land, I remembered the kindness of the officials on both sides who had opened this barbed wire barricade for me, and I wished I had the magic and the wisdom to unite Arab and Jew. Behind me, members of the Arab Legion stood guard; in front of me, the Israeli border patrol kept watch. On one side Arab children played; on the other, Jewish. For Jordanian and Israeli there was no crossing of the line for fear of reprisal, no invasion of a single square foot of this divided Holy Land on fear of death.

I walked, briefcase in hand, wishing for the formula

that could restore to each side a will to believe in the man across the line; and, wishing, I thought of Shoghi Effendi. Did he have the magic word? Could the cause to which he was giving his life, the movement of which he was the supreme head, hold the secret? The word he proclaimed was Baha'i, and in the tense air of silence and suspicion that made this darkening February afternoon more ominous, I found new meaning in the term. Perhaps Baha'i was more than a tag put on a new religion, more than just another promotional movement. The English equivalent of the Persian word *Baha* means light. Shoghi Effendi maintained that it meant light in the sense of knowledge, in the sense of truth, and in the sense of justice. It also meant faith: faith that where God is, there is unity; and God is everywhere.

Baha'i meant a child of light, a follower of Baha'u'llah, the Persian Seer who, in 1863, proclaimed himself the reincarnation of the spirit of Christ. The man I was to see, Shoghi Effendi, was a lineal descendant of Baha'u'llah, and the present Baha'i leader. The million Baha'is in the world affectionately called him the Guardian of their Cause. They were asking Christians to believe that Baha'u'llah was the Comforter whom Jesus had promised to send. They were telling Jews that this new prophet was the one destined to rule upon the throne of David. They were alerting Moslems to the fact that Baha'u'llah had come to quicken and purify their faith. To Zoroastrians they were saying, "He is the Incomparable Friend for whom your people are waiting," and to every great world religion, Baha'is were proclaiming that

Baha'u'llah was the "Lord of Names," the focal point of unity and peace. Baha'u'llah had told the nations, "The earth is one country, and mankind its citizens."

The words seemed incongruous as I walked through the February cold. Heavy hopelessness and bloodshed lay over the land; guards stood on the bombed-out buildings, guns in hand; opposing camps were poised for combat at the slightest border incident. *Baha*—Light—seemed an impossible, unworkable ideal.

Yet, I could not help saying to myself as I thought of Arab and Jew, of East and West, and of nations, races and creeds all over the globe, "Surely there is a belief we hold in common. There is a truth from which we cannot hide. Whatever made us *is* the divine source of every life. In Him we all are one. And if, during this brief and mortal life, we war with one another, we are warring with ourselves and with Him. Light is what we need."

I did not know whether the Arabs behind me, or the Jews toward whom I was making my way, had ever heard about the Baha'is, or whether they knew Shoghi Effendi. And what could I say to them, and to what effect? Could mere words of mine or a Baha'i ideal offer the basis for a practical peace? Two nights ago there had been gunfire. A week ago there had been a border clash and casualties. This was a business of life and death, not a matter of dreams and speculation. What was it the Arab Legionnaire had said at the Jordan border a moment ago when he brought his rubber stamp down on my special papers? "Remember we are at war. You must be back in a week."

"Friday, the thirteenth," I promised.

"Between three and five o'clock," he instructed. "Good-by and good luck to you."

Then, with his two companions, armed, colorful in their red headgear, he had walked with me to the edge of his side of the barbed wire. He had stood there as if envying me my freedom to go—and to return.

Now I was nearing the little shack which served as a shelter for the border patrol of the Israeli government. A young man, bespectacled, stern and strong, leaned out of the shelter and asked me where I was going.

I told him, "Mt. Carmel."

"How do you expect to get by here?" he wanted to know.

I handed him my credentials. He looked them over, then glanced sharply at me, "This doesn't say where you are going."

I said, "I'm on my way to Mt. Carmel."

"And what do you expect to see at Mt. Carmel?"

"Religious shrines."

"Whose shrines?"

"The shrines of many faiths," I told him.

"Ah," he exclaimed, "and what kinds of religions are you interested in?"

"All kinds," I said.

"That's interesting," he replied. "That happens to be my interest, too."

Suddenly he became friendly. He then passed the documents I had given him through a slot in the wall, where a hand took them.

We talked about religion. He told me much about the old faiths, and I told him about the new. And, in passing, I mentioned the Baha'is.

"Ah, you have Baha'is in America?" he asked, and from his tone I was not sure of his attitude, or whether he had more, or less, information about them than I had.

"They have their world-famous temple near Chicago," I informed him. "They call it the Mashriqu'l-Adhkar. It's a great attraction, a new type of architecture. It cost two million dollars. We Americans always like to know what things cost. The temple's nine pylons curve over an alabaster dome. The pylons fuse into one main pinnacle—to show that many paths may lead to God."

When I told him this, he talked about other symbolism: the symbolism of the cabala and also that of Philo of Alexander, the Jewish philosopher, and how, in Philo's hands, Bible characters became dissolved of flesh and blood and took on allegorical meaning.

All this while, I had almost forgotten the papers I had given him, so struck was I by the fact that between us there had grown up a sense of camaraderie. I had never met him before. He had never met me. But we had a common interest: man's eternal quest.

I couldn't help but look back across the desolate stretch of land over which I had come and I think he read my thoughts. But neither of us said anything about that. And finally the hand pushed my papers back through the narrow slot.

The Israeli guard took them. Then he took a rubber stamp in his hand while two men, armed, stood near him, peering over his shoulders.

"Yes," he verified, "everything seems to be in order, though this isn't the way these things are usually done." He brought the stamp down with a bang.

He handed the papers back to me, glanced through my briefcase and added, "We'll expect you back in a week. The gate will be open. It will be open for you between three and five."

I looked toward New Jerusalem, then at him, and reached out my hand to thank him.

He took it and asked, "Are you walking in—all the way?"

"Yes, I guess so. I'm going to the Y. M. C. A. How far is it?"

"Ah, that," he mused, "is a little piece. Maybe I can get you a cab. Would that help you?"

"Yes," I said, "that would be fine."

He took the field telephone and asked that a taxi be sent to take a friend, whom he had just met, into town.

Such kindness had not been shown me—well, not for a while at least—not since I had left the Jordan side.

2.

New Jerusalem, Jaffa, Tel Aviv—cities of the little state of Israel—were teeming with activity and ideas. This new state was like an eager child, trying to absorb everything at once: a way of life in its co-operative ventures, the Kibbutzim; global knowledge in its schools and universities; commerce for world markets in its industries; creative expression in its art and music and manifold manual skills; new agricultural principles in its waterways and irrigation; and a new government spun from the heart of its varied peoples.

Israel was fighting for its life. But on the other side, Jordan was fighting for its life, too. Israel needed food. Jordan had it. Israel had the creative touch; Jordan needed it. Israel wanted to be independent and free. So did Jordan. So did every people. In every country it was always easier to consecrate the fighting spirit than to curb it. It was only a small step from the defense of what was right to the attack of what was wrong. Everywhere in Israel I felt a question, though I did not hear it spoken, "Are you ready to die for your country?" But I was on my way to see Shoghi Effendi who is neither Jew nor Jordanian. He is Persian. He is Baha'i.

I went by way of Akka, for it was in this harbor city that Baha'u'llah, banished from Baghdad, spent his years of exile. Here to this desolate place, where St. Francis of Assisi once walked, Baha'u'llah came in chains in 1865.

I went into what is called the "Most Great Prison" where Baha'u'llah was held captive for twenty-five years, and where his son, Abdul Baha, was a prisoner for forty years. And when I poked around behind these old walls and looked into the dungeons the Baha'i story came to life. Baha'u'llah, like Jesus, had a forerunner who called himself the Bab, which means "the Gate." In the midst of the religious and political squabbles of Moslem, Christian, and Jew the Bab said, in effect, "A plague on all your houses. You have all lost sight of your common origin." He preached that God is the Father of all men and the Founder of all faiths and that the time had come when God would personify this truth. Like John the Baptist, the voice in the wilderness, the Bab announced the coming of another Messiah, Baha'u'llah.

Shoghi Effendi, whom I was to meet, was the eldest son of the eldest daughter of Abdul Baha and a distant relative of the Bab. Abdul Baha had decreed in his will and testment that Shoghi Effendi should carry on the work. At the time of his grandfather's death in 1921, Shoghi was twenty-five and a student at Balliol College, Oxford. He returned at once to Haifa and was enjoined to "live in detachment from all worldly things, be the essence of purity and show in thyself the fear of God, knowledge, wisdom and learning." I was told that all this, too, was contained in the terms of the will.

Long ago in Wilmette, at the door of the Mashriqu'l-Adhkar on Sheridan Road, a woman said to me, "I was in Haifa and saw His Eminence! I have never looked into such eyes in all my life. To obey him is to obey God, and to turn away from him is to turn away from God."

In Chicago, the man who first introduced me to the writings of Shoghi Effendi had said, "Everyone who meets the Guardian is deeply impressed. We are admonished by the will of Abdul Baha to take the greatest possible care of Shoghi Effendi so that 'no dust of despondency and sorrow will stain his radiant nature, and that he may become a fruitful branch on the tree of holiness.' "

In Havana, a Cuban Baha'i told me she believed Shoghi Effendi to be a greater man than Elijah, who vanquished the priests of Baal on the summit of Mt. Carmel.

A professor at the University of Beirut described the Guardian as an artist and a genius; and a Baha'i in Geneva urged me to return that way so that she might "shake the hand that shook the hand of Shoghi Effendi."

From Akka I went to Bahji, some six kilometers inland. Here is the Sheik's mansion where Baha'u'llah lived like a prince following his prison release, and here he died in 1892. Here is the holy spot where Christians, Jews, Moslems, Zoroastrians, and Buddhists came to "lament the loss and magnify the greatness of this herald of God." Baha'is even now do not speak of the death of Baha'u'llah, but, rather, of his ascension.

The taxi driver who took me to this sacred spot let me out at the lane close by an olive grove which might have been another Gethsemane. But on one side were warning signs advising that the Israeli Army had a firing range close by and a camp to which admittance was barred.

I walked through the lane to the big house. In the magnificently landscaped grounds, men were working. They did not look up, so intent were they in making beautiful these gardens of Bahji. I was met by a young man, a Baha'i, who consented to take me into the mansion. He was not interested in my name or nationality. It was enough that I was "seeking", and he concluded in his quiet way that "if one is interested in many religions he cannot help but find his way to the right one."

We took off our shoes at the door which leads to the solemn and beautiful room where Baha'u'llah lies enshrined. For a long while we knelt beside the bier. My companion prayed and I fell to wondering at how many other shrines were worshipers saying their prayers at this very moment. In every country, no matter how torn by war, or how divided by man hating man, voices were being raised to heaven by way of prophets and messiahs. In caves and cathedrals, in tombs and temples, these everlasting chants were going on and just how or when this cacophony concerning the Fatherhood of God could ever be transposed into the harmony of the Brotherhood of Man was a mystery. It was a mystery for me, but not for the Baha'is. They simply said that this question had been answered when Baha'u'llah came into the world, and would be fulfilled when the world came to Baha'-u'llah.

So I walked through the majestic rooms with my guide who regarded with reverence every book and tablet, every picture and place with which the Splendor of God had once been associated. In a large, rectangular parlor, along one side of which ran a low divan and where prayer rugs were now in evidence, I was reminded that it was here the noted Cambridge University Orientalist, Professor Edward G. Browne, visited Baha'u'llah. His impressions were widely quoted, and a commentary, known from memory by every ardent Baha'i, reported, "The face of him on whom I gazed I can never forget, though I cannot describe it. Those piercing eyes seemed to read one's very soul; power and authority sat on that ample brow; while the deep lines on the forehead and face implied an age which the jet-black hair and beard, flowing down in indistinguishable luxuriance almost to his waist, seemed to belie. No need to ask in whose presence I stood, as I bowed myself before One who is the object of a devotion and love which kings might envy and emperors sigh for in vain!"

This, many Baha'is had warned me, was only a foreshadowing of what I would say when I met the present leader, Shoghi Effendi.

"Do you want to see him?" my guide whispered.

"Who?"

"The Guardian? Shoghi Effendi? He is here on the grounds. Come here to the window. Ah, you cannot see him because he is surrounded by the workmen out there."

"I am meeting him tonight," I stated.

The Baha'i turned to me as if he must have misunderstood.

"I beg your pardon?" he managed to say.

"I have an appointment with him tonight at Haifa."

"You mean—personally?" He looked me over as if for the first time. "He is expecting you?"

"Yes. Those are the arrangements."

"He seldom grants interviews." His voice was still suspicious. "He has never been to America. He writes as Baha'u'llah writes, to draw men to God. He plans as Abdul Baha planned, for world citizenship. He works so that God's kingdom should come on earth as it is in heaven."

With these prophetic words ringing in my ears I returned to the lane close by the olive trees, made my way on foot back to Akka, and there caught a bus for Haifa.

3.

The Guardian's home is under the watchful shadow of Mt. Carmel. On this green and holy hill, which Isaiah compared to the beauty of the Kingdom of God, Elijah taught his disciples. Here Pythagoras came to meditate; here Napoleon founded a hospital; and saints and martyrs built their grottos and chose their graves. And here Baha'u'llah made his retreats and proclaimed that Haifa should be the fountainhead of the Baha'i Cause.

The Baha'i shrine on Mt. Carmel has the jewel-like perfection of the Taj Mahal. Its great pillars face Haifa harbor, as if Baha'u'llah's prophecy was being forced to come true; "A person standing on the summit of Mt. Carmel, and the passengers on the steamers coming to it, will look upon the most sublime and majestic spectacle of the whole world." Inside the granite walls of this "Blessed Tomb" lie the remains of the Bab and the body of Abdul Baha.

When I arrived at 10 Persian Street, the quiet thoroughfare that leads up to the sacred mount, I was welcomed into a pleasant room in Pilgrim House, just across from the Guardian's residence, by Ethel Revell, a secretary on the Baha'i international staff.

"His Eminence will be with us for dinner," she said, and looked at me as if trying to determine whether or not I realized what an honor was being accorded me.

Ethel Revell was typically a Baha'i, full of enthusiasm, tireless in her desire to talk about the Guardian, and leaving no doubt that she had at last found the faith to which she could unselfishly devote her life. But I was wrong in my impression that she was in her "first love" or that she was a recent convert to the cause. Her identity with the movement went back to her girlhood in Philadelphia forty years ago when her mother had introduced her to Abdul Baha, then touring the United States. The bearded white patriarch took her in his arms and prophesied that she would one day be close to the heart of the work.

She and her sister, Jessie, had come to Haifa in 1945 to work as zealots in the Guardian's community, asking no financial compensation and having no desire for any earthly acclaim. After eight years in this service, they still found that nothing had grown commonplace. Haifa was still the most vibrant spot on earth, because the Guardian was here. The work was the most satisfying in all the world, because his spirit made it so. The privilege of service was a cherished one, because any of the one million Baha'is in the Cause would count it an honor to be close to the "source of Light."

"You are highly favored," she reminded me. "After you have seen the Guardian you will never be the same."

The words had a familiar ring.

Whatever kind of man he was, he had drawn together into one procession many races, creeds, and minds. Great people and little people were marching with him toward the citadel of a united world. Rich and poor were finding a common ground, in sentiment, at least. Strong and weak were joining hands and hearts in an ideal. His Eminence was leading them onward to what he called a "world-girding mission" and they knew what this meant.

It meant that the temple at Ishquabad behind the Iron Curtain was a symbol of free men in a faithless land. It meant that the Mashriqu'l-Adhkar at Wilmette enunciated the spirit of the Baha'i community in the Western Hemisphere. It meant that the missionary activity in Africa, India, and Asia was conducted not by a paid clergy, but by volunteers who unselfishly gave their time and fortunes to the Cause. It meant shrines at Akka and Bahji and Mt. Carmel. It meant the hour had come for the fulfillment of the beatitude of Baha'u'llah, "Blessed are they who shall proclaim the doctrine of spiritual brotherhood, for they shall be called the Children of Light!"

While I was visualizing these things and while Miss Revell was telling me how marvelously the Baha'i faith recommended itself for our time, the door opened and a trim, attractive woman entered, suddenly and unannounced. She had a dog on a leash, a fur stole around her neck, and she walked like a Persian queen. Only she was American, at least I thought she was, and the piquancy with which she came in must have pleased or shocked the spirits of the old prophets who haunted the mansion room.

She made herself comfortable in a chair and said, "So. Tell me about yourself. You are interested in religions.

What have you found in all this searching?"

This was a surprise approach. Most Baha'is started out by telling me what they had found. Generally their aim was to convince me at once of the worth of the Cause. What kind of a zealot was this who invited me to present my case?

I reviewed the list of groups that had come under my study and when I explained that there always seemed to me to be a greater common ground for understanding than for differences, she voiced her agreement.

"Religions," she said, "are not parallel lines. They are bound to meet. Each is the expression of something vital that people have found in their search."

As she went on in this vein, she still made no mention of the Baha'is or of Baha'u'llah or of the Guardian. Who was this woman, and why did not Miss Revell introduce me? Perhaps she didn't have a chance, for the stranger was weaving a mood that did not admit of any rude intrusion.

"Each faith draws upon the inner well of experience," she mused. "In each there is something beautiful and disciplined and prophetic. The great religions *are* leaves of the same tree. The thinking person can and must find harmony among all true prophets and unity in all true scriptures."

She talked as though time and conversation were intended for the deepening of knowledge and faith. And I noticed another thing: she spoke in the lyrical, poetic style of Baha'u'llah himself, and it was difficult to tell which thoughts were hers and which were his. It was Baha'i philosophy to be sure, but it was presented as though it were her own.

"You know," she was saying, "a believer in the Unity of God must recognize in every created thing the evidence of the revelation of God. The creature is not indistinguishable from the Creator. Those who recognize the Unity of God are the primary revealers of God."

How we got so swiftly from my research into her discovery, I never quite knew. I think it must have been the fault of the dog. He was a shaggy, loveable fellow and somewhere along the way I commented on him. I think it was then she said something about feeling and sensitivity being the hallmarks of living matter and how much higher these qualities should be in human beings than in dogs. The greater the person, the more he should realize that he does not stand alone; that he draws upon the hidden resources of the spirit.

At some length she expounded the benefits to be derived by people who face the burdens and blows of life, for these can change weaklings into persons of strength. She believed, also, that this principle of rigorous discipline applies in the animal world. Her dog, now, she was sure, would be much better behaved had she been less lenient in her training of him.

Then she spoke of life's joy and triumphs, and of what happens to the individual when God becomes real to him, and he enters the orb of spiritual experience. The quest kindles the fire; faith lights it.

She touched on many other things of a similar nature, such as sorrow and suffering, which seemed to her to be part of the spiritual process. Of suffering she said, "I do not know the why of it, but I know that every time I have suffered I have grown in spirit and felt refined."

It was during one of these rapidly paced impressions, when I felt the spirits of the prophets had turned the tables on me and were using her as their mouthpiece, that I said, "I hope I'm not being too inquisitive, but with whom do I have the honor of visiting?"

"Oh," she said with a slight laugh, while her hand gently stroked the dog's head, "my history is brief. I was born in Canada. My people were Baha'is and a few years ago it was my great privilege to become the wife of the Guardian."

I was frankly surprised and felt moved to exclaim, I didn't know the Guardian was married. How does all his reputed greatness seem to you, his wife? Why is it that in Baha'i circles we do not hear more about you? Instead, I merely said, "I am very happy to meet you."

"Thank you," was the gracious reply. "We shall be together at dinner in a little while."

Then she went out, taking the dog with her for a walk.

4.

Shoghi Effendi did not come for the evening meal. He telephoned his regrets, explaining that he had been delayed at Bahji. He assured me that immediately after dinner he would meet me in his home, but his absence from our little gathering was the cause of keen disappointment for the five guests and for Madame Rabbani, as the wife of the Guardian is known.

"He works tirelessly," she said.

"He will be with us in spirit," said one of the women.

So we went into the pleasant basement dining room at Pilgrim House. Madame Rabbani sat at one end of the large table and I at the other. At her right was Dr. Lotfullah S. Hakim, an elderly Persian physician and close personal friend of the Guardian. Next to him was Mrs. Amelia Collins, a prominent American Baha'i. At my right were the Revell sisters and Mrs. Sylvia Ioas, wife of the secretary of the Baha'i Spiritual Assembly.

As a maid and helper in Pilgrim House came in with a tray of food, Madame Rabbani asked me to speak a word of prayer. The tempting aroma of Persian cooking persuaded me to thank the Lord for the universality of food as well as faith. I expressed gratitude, too, for the spirit of the Baha'i Cause and for every attempt that aids man in his search for truth and peace.

No doubt a menu of curried chicken, rice pilaf, chutney, oven roasted peanuts, and fried bananas would put anyone in a receptive mood for almost any kind of table talk. But as the meal progressed, I found more convincing answers to my questions about the Baha'i movement than any previously supplied. For one thing, I learned through Madame Rabbani and Dr. Hakim, that prayer and the earnest practice of the presence of God are basic in the faith. I was informed that a Baha'i is not a true Baha'i unless a consciousness of God is effected within him by the age-old formula, known to every seeker as "waiting upon God." This meant meditation, contemplation, reflection.

I was sure that many people in the traditional churches were of the opinion that Baha'ism was more sociological than spiritual. Most of my Protestant and Catholic friends considered it a glorified fraternal order with a utopian dream about making the whole world one native land. Here in the heart of Haifa, at this pleasant table, I came to realize that the religion of Baha'u'llah is interested in an inner personal development as well as in a global plan, and I concluded the latter would be unrealizable unless the former were first attained.

"You cannot change the world without first changing the individual," was the formula, and never before had this point been driven home despite my many meetings with Baha'is in other lands.

It became clear to me, as I was sure it must have been to other pilgrims whose paths have led them to 10 Persian Street, that a true Baha'i should live the life of a contemplative and should seek, as the wife of the Guardian earnestly declared, "that unity and peace in his own life which he hopes to see manifested in the world."

To the serene and quiet-spoken Dr. Hakim, Shoghi Effendi was an object of veneration. He had a fatherly affection for the Baha'i leader and a watchfulness that seemed commissioned to guard not only his health but his spirit. It was Shoghi Effendi who had persuaded the doctor that: "there are two ways of healing the sick: material means and spiritual means. The first is through material remedies. The second is through praying to God and turning to Him."

The prayers the doctor prayed were also those of the Guardian:

O God! Thy nearness is my hope,
And to commune with Thee, my joy;
Thy love is my comfort
And Thy Name, my prayer.

My estimate of Shoghi Effendi grew because of the words and devotion of Mirza Hakim. It was he who assured me that this holy man of Haifa had outlined the plan for the Baha'i commonwealth and had given the world the widest and most comprehensive idea of the heroism of faith. It was he who was teaching men how to live in truth and righteousness and in harmony with the Spirit of God.

To Dr. Hakim and to the pilgrims on Persian Street, Shoghi Effendi was a prophet. Their continual references to his work, his writings, and his power made me impatient for my meeting with him.

5.

It was nine o'clock when I walked with Madame Rabbani to the Guardian's home. Lights had appeared on

Mt. Carmel and a path of lights led up to the sacred shrine. The air was crisp and fragrant. Silence hung over the city and far in the distance the beacon from a signal tower flashed and faded in its circular flight, bringing to mind the Baha'i symbol of the reappearance of light in prophetic cycles.

Madame Rabbani ushered me into a large, sparsely furnished room. She said she would see whether His Eminence was now ready to see me. Would I mind waiting?

The room was filled with haunting sensations: the fragrance of incense; a sense of something mysterious; the peaceful lingering of the night outside the open door, in sharp contrast with the unrest and fear that everywhere seemed to brood over Palestine.

Through an inner door which stood open, I could see a spacious adjoining room, also meagerly furnished but majestic. Near me on the wall was a framed page from the writings of Abdul Baha. This, aside from an Oriental wall hanging, was the only decoration.

I walked the heavily carpeted floor with a sudden rush of questions. Why, I asked myself, accept a new prophet when we have not yet lived the principles and teachings of the old? Had not Jesus beleaguered us with more challenges for life than we could ever satisfactorily meet? Had He not already told us to love our fellowmen and our neighbors as ourselves? And we had not yet come around to that. How, then, could we possibly create a new world order?

This new religion was also asking us to accept Baha'-u'llah before we had made our peace with Krishna and Zoroaster and Mohammed and the Divine Manifestations of other faiths. Would not every organized religious movement see in Baha'u'llah a threat its own messiah, rather than a blessing to all mankind?

I wondered, too, while waiting for Shoghi Effendi, whether we could ever accept all Scriptures as holy, as the Baha'is requested. We Christians were still arguing about the Bible. We were still buying Bibles without reading them and reading them without knowing what was meant. We were even re-translating our Holy Book, deleting passages here and there and changing the meaning of basic texts! Were we ready, then, to accept the Scripture of Baha'u'llah?

But I kept thinking, What must it be like to find a faith that answers all one's questions; to discover one single, satisfying institutionalized expression and to say, "Now I need search no longer. Here is everything I have been looking for!"

How could this ever be possible? What would happen to the individual then? What would happen to me if I were suddenly to say, "This is it! My search is over! Here in the Baha'i mecca, I have found the Pearl of Great Price!"

Madame Rabbani was standing, tall and poised, in the doorway.

"He will be here in a moment," she announced. "I am sure you are going to enjoy your visit with him very much."

There was no doubting her sincerity or her enthusiasm. In a glance, warm and friendly, she seemed to be saying, "There was a time when I was seeking just as you are. I was looking for something, too, something to which I could really consecrate my life."

Then I saw coming through the adjoining room a small, dark-complexioned man, dressed in Western attire but wearing a fez. His clean-shaven face and slender figure registered indomitable strength. He walked with head up as though an entourage of the faithful might be following him. He strode in, bowed to me with an almost imperceptible nod, and held out his hand. As we exchanged greetings there was a smile on his lips, though this did not entirely destroy my impression of a certain aloofness in his bearing. He welcomed me with a sensitivity that seemed to feel, rather than hear my words.

The expression of his dark eyes, too, gave a hint of inner judgment based not on what was said but, rather, on what was sensed. He was self-possessed, self-sufficient, purposeful. I had been told he was a man of fifty-seven, but, judging from his unlined, youthful face, he might have been only forty. And though I stood head and shoulders above him, I felt diminutive. I envied him the sense of security and holy mission in life that filled his whole soul with confidence, beyond doubt and beyond question.

He looked at me steadily for a moment as if to determine whether I was truly a pilgrim or whether I had dropped around for sensational information about what I might lightly consider the rise and romance of another sect. Apparently satisfying himself that he would never have been led to keep this interview unless God had sent me, he directed me with a nod and a gesture to a chair. He took his place on a divan and as he put into words the thoughts I had already divined, he smiled knowingly. Had I come all this distance only to ask the general run of questions? What was the purpose of my visit?

My first few words, "an interest in religion that has deepened into a quest," brought a quick nod of understanding. It was almost as if I had made an electrical contact. His eyes flashed. Ah, yes, he knew what I meant. A man could not seek long in the jungle of religions without wanting to find a good trail, a way out, a way toward the light. Light was what men needed. How restless the world! How caught in its many complexities! How desperately men needed the new message, the good message that the kingdoms of the earth are passing away and the kingdom of God is in the making.

Quietly he took me at once into the heart of the Baha'i Cause and though I had heard much of this before from members of the faith, it was a new experience for me to meet a religious leader who was not defending one Book, but, rather, Books; who had no argument for one Messiah, but for Messiahs; who was not pointing out one way, but ways, to God.

"The faith identified with the name of Baha'u'llah disclaims any intent to belittle any of the Prophets gone before Him, to whittle down any of their teachings, to obscure, however slightly, the radiance of their revelations or oust them from the hearts of their followers, to abrogate the fundamentals of their doctrines, to discard any of their revealed Books, or to suppress the legitimate aspirations of their adherents.

"Repudiating the claim of any religion to be the final revelation of God to man, thus disclaiming finality for his own revelation, Baha'u'llah inculcates the basic principle of the relativity of religious truth, the oneness of Divine Revelation, and religious experience. His aim is to widen the basis of all revealed religions and to unravel the mysteries of their scriptures. . . . He separates the God-given truths from the priest-prompted superstitions, and on this basis proclaims the possibility, and prophesies the inevitability, of their unification and the consummation of their highest hopes."

This is how he described the Baha'i Cause and how he presented it to me. This was "the continuity of revelation" and he was an instrument in the process. Baha'u'llah had brought the message. He, the Guardian, was implementing it into the unification of all mankind.

6.

This, then, was the man I had come to see, a beardless prophet, one who might have been a successful businessman, artist, or teacher; an intense and vital man, whose all-seeing eyes always read my thoughts in advance, whose sharp mind had a ready answer the moment my questions were asked.

"Is the Baha'i faith really making an impact upon the world?" I asked.

"Religious revolution, social evolution stand at the door of our age," he proclaimed. "The dynasties of institutionalized religion and centralized political power are confounded by the Light of the Cause. A new world civilization is being born, a new day is dawning."

"But do you think the world is really more religious than it has been? Is it more spiritually inclined . . . ?"

"Man has let go of God but God will not let go of man. Religions must face each other honestly. Let them recognize the Faith and the Prophet that can unite them. Men have been so absorbed in the study of theology that they have neglected the study of life."

His words were sparks thrown from the anvil of the Bab—rays of light from the torch of Baha'u'llah. These masters had dared accuse kings and priests of wresting power from God. They had foretold the fearful penalties of such ambition, and the Guardian described what these penalties were: the collapse of organized religion, the crumbling of ecclesiasticism, strife within Christendom, the disintegration of world powers, the rise of "the triple false gods of Nationalism, Racialism and Communism."

Had I not read about the fate of empires which had rejected the counsel of Baha'u'llah? Shrunken and extinguished they had become! He had written about this in *The Promised Day is Come*. He had stated the facts for all the world to see.

"Consider the fate of the Napoleonic, the Romanov,

the Hohenzollren, the Hapsburg empires, which, together with the sovereign occupant of the Papal throne, were individually addressed by Baha'u'llah! What of France whose emperor flung away Baha'u'llah's Tablet? What of the fate that has overtaken the Chinese Empire, the Portuguese and Spanish monarchies? What of England? Did not Queen Victoria, upon reading the Tablet sent to her, remark, 'If this is of God, it will endure; if not, it can do no harm?' What of Russia which Baha'u'llah had warned never to turn from the face of God? What of the Holy Roman Empire?" Baha'u'llah had written his warning and it was unheeded. Then, in his lifetime the virtual extinction of the temporal sovereignty of the Supreme Pontiff was held up for all the world to see.

He spoke like that, in words tinged with poetry and power. He spoke in melodious, faultless English, with a firm and stanch authority as if what he had to say was said by divine right. He blended the vast run of world events for the past century into the hub of the 1863 proclamation that Baha'u'llah had come to do God's work and will.

I was assured that a blueprint for global unity existed in the writings of Baha'u'llah and Abdul Baha, that every emergence of a plan for universal order, from the League of Nations to the United Nations, had received its inspiration from this source; and that these were rays of light emanating from the brilliance that came from the Baha'i world.

"But how," I asked, "do you account for the fact that

the faith has not grown more rapidly than it has? There are not more than ten or twelve thousand Baha'is in the United States."

"Our influence cannot be counted in numbers," he declared. "But the Baha'i world population is very large and very strong."

"Christian Science," I made bold to say, "which also goes back to approximately 1863, has at least half a million members in America. The Adventists, who go back about a hundred years, number some 300,000. Jehovah's Witnesses have about 500,000. These groups have all sprung up during the past century."

"The trouble with these new religions," came his considered reply, "is that they are always offering the people something. People too often join a new religion, or even an old one, because they expect to get something out of it. Baha'is believe they have something to *give*."

He contended that the westernization of the Christian faith tended to make it opportunistic. "The western concept is, 'What can I get out of religion? What is in it for me?' The Baha'i religion asks, 'What am I willing to give?' What did the first followers of Jesus expect to get out of the Christian faith? A cross."

I had no doubt that he, too, would be willing to carry a cross for his belief. He had no other purpose than to see his mission accomplished. Build the faith! Complete the shrines! Guard and guide the people! Resist the enemies of the Cause! Trust in God! The divan on which he sat might have been a throne; his words, the words of a king.

But the thing that struck me most as our meeting progressed was his unquestioned devotion to the Galilean. He was fully as faithful to Jesus as he was to Baha'u'llah. Any basis for understanding the Baha'i concept would have to start with the premise that Shoghi Effendi was a thorough-going Christian in the philosophical, if not in the theological, sense. In fact, the true Baha'i had to be as much or more of a Christian than the Christian himself. This new faith was no less than a fulfillment of the promise given by Christ that the kingdom He had prayed for was now being established. It was Jesus, not Baha'u'llah or, perhaps, Jesus incarnated in Baha'u'llah who claimed first attention in the Cause—and also in this interview which was continued far into the night.

The knowledge, love, and commitment which Shoghi Effendi held for Jesus were a startling revelation. Through Him he had become the recipient of a religious stability and power that put me to shame. Jesus was surely, truly, undebatably, the Chosen of God. What would happen if we would really follow Him? The sword would be put away. The guns would be silenced. Men would be kind and humble in spirit, mighty in purpose.

To the Guardian the relationship between Jesus and Baha'u'llah was consistently unvarying. The world, he recalled, had rejected the Christ. It was again seeking to reject the Splendor of God. But as the Prophet of Nazareth seized and conquered the minds of men, so the Prophet of Teheran was conquering, too. As the Prince of Peace shook and terrified the kingdoms of selfish individuals, so the Prince of Unity was even now beginning to shatter the kingdoms of selfish systems. Jesus and Baha'u'llah were Divine Manifestations, whole and inseparable.

And so I learned that while a fearful condemnation hung over those who rejected and persecuted the Christ, an equally terrible judgment rested upon those who would reject and deny the Persian Seer.

Speaking of life and work, the Guardian said, "The individual has two wings: knowledge and faith. When these are in perfect co-ordination, the soul rises to divine perfection."

Concerning the relationship between science and religion, he observed, "Religion has erred in that it has made an adversary of science. True religion and true science are not natural enemies; rather, they are partners in revealing the presence of God."

Evil, he called a lack of good; darkness, an absence of light; and both, veils which hide the truth from men who seek it. Why men love evil more than good, and why they seek darkness rather than light, are among life's mysteries. There are other mysteries: the reason for suffering and the end of God's plan for the earth.

But why, Shoghi Effendi wondered, should the individual ever feel impatient or driven, or why should he lose his sense of balance? Such conditions are attributable only to a lack of faith and trust. Let those who love the Light never be shaken by these circumstances. Let them never be blinded. Let them remember that civilization is like a growing person and that distresses, disturbances, and tensions are factors in the upward climb. Human life is very young. Civilization is an adolescent—a delinquent adolescent at that—but it is God's child and God will see that it reaches the full stature of man.

He spoke of life after death. Baha'u'llah's teachings in this respect were worthy of being stated as a fundamental creed: "Know of a truth that the soul, after its separation from the body, will continue to progress until it attains the presence of God, in a state and condition which neither the revolution of ages and centuries, nor the changes and chances of this world can alter."

The greatest forces in the world, he assured me, are the prophets of God. Through them God makes Himself known and carries civilization forward. They are His messengers. They live, and it is God living among men. They speak, and it is God's word. They suffer, and it is God bearing the pain and the sin of the world. They take upon themselves disdain and persecution, and it is God bowing His head and baring His shoulders to the whips and scourges of his children. They die, and it is God who weeps. They ascend, and it is God in His glory who again shows man His true estate.

The moments went by. The hour grew late. I had a notebook in my pocket but I did not open it that night. It might have helped me to remember his words, but not his faith. That was something to be felt and cherished. His awareness of God was paramount. With him, all is God's will and the Prophets have so revealed it. All is God's work and that is what the Prophets have proclaimed. Everything is God. Everything is known to God, whether it be a nation that disappears or a sparrow that falls.

7.

It was near midnight when the Guardian rose to his feet. He extended his hand, and expressed the hope that we would meet again. Then he turned and walked to the door, through the adjoining room, and out of sight as if the retinue of followers marched in triumphal procession behind him.

Out in the moonlit street I gazed up at the silhouetted shrine on the green hill that is Mt. Carmel. Catholicism has Rome. Islam has Mecca. Protestantism has it claim on Bethlehem. The Jew has Jerusalem. The Baha'i has his holy hill in Haifa. Here is the focal point. Here, in the making, is an amalgam of religions based upon blending the divine pronouncements of all traditional religions into an administrative order vested in the Guardian. Could Mt. Carmel, God's throne, make the world its footstool?

In my room in Pilgrim House a bowl of fruit had been set on the table, together with several books on philosophy and religion. There were also Shoghi Effendi's English translations of the writings of Baha'u'llah and a recently published volume, *Prescription for Living,* by Madame Rabbani. Its theme was a dramatic reminder of her conviction that the fate of tomorrow's world is dependent upon the disposition we make of the new world faith today.

This book's theme and the Guardian's pronouncements had charge of my thoughts for most of the following days, especially on that Friday, the thirteenth, when, between the hours of three and five, I was back in Jerusalem and at the Mandelbaum Gate. Could the spiritual light which Shoghi Effendi kept burning ever unite Arab and Jew? Could it bring peace to the divided Holy Land or to any land where armies stood along disputed borders? Adolescent the world might now be; but would it ever be mature enough to agree that God's chosen people include all mankind?

I thought about Shoghi Effendi. In a divided world his voice rose with great conviction: there can be no peace until force gives way to faith and terrorism to trust; there can be no unity until individuals make the words of Baha'u'llah the law of the land, "Let not a man glory in this, that he loves his country, let him rather glory in this, that he loves his kind."

There was no mystery or question about the source of the Guardian's strength. The reason for his influence was clear. There was a time when his path crossed the path of the Man from Nazareth. And when these paths crossed, he made a disposition of the Nazarene. He made of Him a Prophet—a Prophet with honor in Palestine, a Prophet with honor throughout the world.

That was it. He was part of the circle of faith. His arc was the arc of prophecy. I remembered how, on the day following our interview, we walked the sacred Baha'i grounds on Mt. Carmel. I would always remember how he pointed out the yet unfinished plan for building, how he emphasized that "This must be because it is so ordered" and that "Here it is ordained that this should be completed." There is always One standing with him. It is the spirit of the Prophet.

Had Shoghi Effendi lived at the time of Jesus he would have read a prophetic meaning into all of the Master's words. In each beatitude he would have found a hidden implication, in each injunction a foreshadowing of event following upon event, in each intimate conversation a hint of things to come. He would have been the first among the disciples to recognize Jesus as God's Prophet and not merely as a prophet of God.

Christ, for Shoghi Effendi, is "all Prophet." Had Shoghi lived in the time of Jesus this recognition would have ruled and guided his life then, as it rules and guides his life today. Without this awareness, he could not have believed in Baha'u'llah. With it, his life, his fate, his will are bound up with his implicit trust in the prophetic elements of the Messianic concept.

In the heat of theological speculation that seeks to divide Jesus into a thousand parts and even divides Him against Himself, Shoghi Effendi stands secure and unshaken in what he considers his divine impression. His path crossed the path of Jesus and he made of Him a Prophet. Is it right? Is it wrong? Is it swindle or miracle, false or true?

It is simply the instinctive response of a distinctive nature, the concentration of the entire devotion on the Absolute Godhead and the assurance that at times this Godhead descends into human form. His path crossed the path of Jesus and he made of Him a Prophet.

He has that type of mind.

4.

HELEN KELLER

1.

And there was Helen Keller.

Her photograph hung in my boyhood school. Still lingering in my memory is this picture of a woman holding an open book; a woman who seemed to stand adventurously and fearlessly before the world. But I knew that the book she held was in raised print to be read only by the blind.

Though Helen Keller was not yet forty in those days, she was already a legend. We had to learn certain facts about her story: that she was born on June 27, 1880, in Tuscumbia, Alabama; that her father was editor of the local newspaper; that she had been a normal child at birth, but had lost both sight and hearing at the age of nineteen months, the result of an illness.

Just what this meant—to be robbed of seeing the world and hearing its sounds—was impressed upon us by our teacher. She had seen Helen Keller. She had watched as Miss Keller "listened" to music by placing her hand on the vibrating piano and "listened" to speech by touching her fingers to the speaker's lips.

We were told that every letter, every syllable and word that this remarkable woman spoke had been learned through the sense of touch. It had been necessary for her to "read" the movement of the throat, lips, and tongue of her teacher in order to fashion her words. Over and over, day after day, year after year, this blind and deaf girl had unceasingly practiced the sounds. In this way she had learned to speak not only English, but French and German, too, and, our teacher hinted, Greek and Latin as well.

These graphic accounts, transmitted to me at an impressionable age, made the woman with the book an amazing and solitary figure. Tantalizing me was the disconcerting thought that my own sight and hearing—which I took for granted—were insecure and precarious possessions, treasures which an unseen force could suddenly snatch away, and I often wondered about the love and character of God.

Sometimes, recounting what our teacher had told us about Helen Keller, we youngsters would close our eyes and stop up our ears to try to feel or sense what it would be like to live in a sightless and soundless world. How far could we walk without becoming frightened? How much could we "feel" of what was being said by holding our fingers to the lips of the speaker? We always assured ourselves that we could see and hear again. Helen Keller couldn't.

Her autobiography became our text. To me it was a spiritualized Horatio Alger story and I combed it for clues to the many questions that even my teacher could not answer or explain: Why had this happened to Helen Keller? Was it an act of God? Were there many others like her in the world? And most of all, what some of us wanted to know, and talked about among ourselves, was what goes on in a person's heart when one is blind and deaf? What does one think about God? How does one keep from becoming bitter and sorry for oneself and from hating everyone who has eyes that see and ears that hear?

Blindness and deafness were hard facts. But the power to conquer them, instead of letting them conquer you, was becoming a fact, too. Of this, Helen Keller was the great example. There was, then, evidently something within a person which was unwilling to surrender no matter how great the problem or how fierce the handicap. And I would look at the picture again, the picture of the woman with the book, looking serenely at the world though she saw only darkness and heard no sound. Could it be that we who had none of these physical handicaps needed the faith she had found? Could it be that we, too, often walked in darkness, wanting light, and lived in a soundless world, longing to hear a voice?

We were told that the coming of a teacher, Anne Sullivan, into Helen Keller's life, was like the coming of a presence. This had a vague meaning and a symbolism dimly grasped.

"On the afternoon of that eventful day," Helen Keller wrote in *The Story of My Life,* "I stood on the porch, dumb, expectant. I guessed vaguely from my mother's signs and from the hurrying to and fro in the house that something unusual was about to happen, so I went to the door and waited on the steps. . . . Have you ever been at sea in a dense fog, when it seemed as if a tangible white darkness shut you in, and the great ship, tense and anxious, groped her way toward the shore . . . and you waited with beating heart for something to happen? I was like that ship, only I was without compass or sounding line, and had no way of knowing how near the harbour was. 'Light! Give me light!' was the wordless cry of my soul, and the light of love shone on me in that very hour."

We who read these words, absorbing the inner expression, feeling the groping of the imprisoned spirit, we who sat in a class taught by one who had "really seen Helen Keller," felt that the shadow of legend was taking on a form of reality.

Anne Sullivan—who was later to become Anne Sullivan Macy—was twenty when she came to the Keller home. Partially blind, she had entered the Perkins Institution for the Blind in Boston and had been recommended to the Kellers by the Institution's director, Michael Anagnos.

Anne came to Tuscumbia bearing as a gift a doll from the blind children at the Institution. When she presented it to Helen she spelled the word "d-o-l-l" manually into her pupil's hand. This was the first word Helen had ever "felt." She was fascinated, but only because it seemed to her a game. She did not know that the cloth-covered thing she held in her arms, a thing which had the outline of a face and body, was related in any way to the rhythmic motion of her teacher's fingers.

Anne Sullivan taught her other signs for other things. But one day during the spelling game, Helen resisted, puzzled. Her sightless eyes were fixed and cold as if her world had become even more insecure. What did "d-o-l-l" mean? What was she to understand by it? Who or what could tell her? Confused and agonized, she flew into a violent rage, flung the doll to the floor and angrily stomped among the broken pieces.

Then, one day her cry for "Light!" was answered. She had walked with her teacher to the pump-house, carrying a cup. The warmth of the sun, the scent of honeysuckles, the feeling of life pulsing about her in the world—not unlike the life that throbbed in her—caused her to hold the cup under the spout thoughtfully.

As the water filled it and rushed over her fingers, Miss Sullivan spelled "w-a-t-e-r" into her free hand. She repeated the manual letters over and over, and with the making of them the spirit of the teacher said to the spirit of her pupil, "This is *water*. What you are feeling has a name. The name is *water*. Everything has a name. This is *water . . . water . . .*"

Helen stood still. A tremor passed through her. Her attention was fixed upon the motion of her teacher's fingers desperately spelling w-a-t-e-r, while cool on her hand was the water from the well.

Suddenly a light broke over her face. Her eyes seemed touched with life. She dropped the cup and with her fingers spelled "water" again and again. Then she fell to the ground and made ecstatic, eager signs demanding the name for the pump, the trellis, the flowers and, turning upon Miss Sullivan asked to know Anne's name. Anne Sullivan spelled "t-e-a-c-h-e-r" into Helen's hand.

Then they stood together: the pupil and the "presence." They stood together in the brightness of "the light." Our teacher said it was a miracle. But this was not easy for us to understand. Was it not true that Helen's eyes were still blind and her ears still deaf? Then we listened while she read a letter which Miss Sullivan had written to a friend on the day after the "miracle" in which she said:

"Helen got up this morning like a radiant fairy. She has flitted from object to object, asking the name of everything and kissing me for very gladness. Last night when I got in bed, she stole into my arms of her own accord and kissed me for the first time. I thought my heart would burst, so full was it of joy."

So we saw with youthful vision the unfolding of something within a person which became fully as real, and fully as mysterious, as the unfolding of life itself. We sensed some of the deeper meaning dimly, and I, for one, never thought about Helen Keller without thinking about God. It may be that her picture still hangs in that little Wisconsin school, for through the years she has walked in the world as one of our greatest contemporaries.

2.

There was one other incident which caused the blind-deaf girl of Tuscumbia to assume unusual spiritual dimensions early in my life. An aunt of mine, afflicted with an incurable goiter, had a saying when friends pitied her, "Remember Helen Keller."

I associated her fortitude with faith and her faith with

the faith of Helen Keller. God, apparently, did lay a "cross" upon certain people. One had to, at times, take literally the saying, "Whom the Lord loveth He chastenth." And in an effort to resolve some of my questions about suffering, Aunt Selma had a stubborn argument straight out of scripture. There was, after all, a blind man in Jesus' time and some people then, even as some of us moderns, demanded the why of it. "Who has sinned? This man or his parents?" And Jesus replied that in this case no one had sinned. The man was blind so that the glory of God might be revealed.

That is how my aunt explained a spiritual mystery to me and that, I felt sure, was how she felt about her own peculiar place in the good Lord's scheme of things. That is how she felt about Helen Keller's place in the world. To Aunt Selma, Miss Keller was far from legendary. She was as real as though she lived next door. I was assured that no one needed to pity her for she was quite capable of making her way in life, having been able to match wits with Mark Twain and hold her own with Oliver Wendell Holmes. She had met all of the Presidents from the time of Theodore Roosevelt and when President Wilson asked her why she had gone to Radcliffe College she replied, "Because they did not want me there. And I am stubborn and had made up my mind to go."

My aunt had seen Helen Keller in the 1920s—in vaudeville. Miss Keller was there not as an exhibit or sensation, but as an envoy for the blind and deaf who wanted not pity but a place in life.

There was a certain symbolism in this vaudeville performance if one cared to look for it. In the midst of jugglers and animal acts and dance teams and what-not, there came to the stage this heroine of the handicapped. She brought to the audience a sudden quiet, proving at once that every person is dual in nature, and transformed for a brief moment, the theater into a chapel, proving, too, that physical surroundings are but an echo of the human heart.

Anne Sullivan Macy was with her. She told the story of how Helen learned to speak and of how until she was ten she had made only harsh, meaningless noises. She described the incident at the pump-house and explained how Helen's speech had been developed by Sarah Fuller of the Horace Mann School for the Deaf in Boston. Miss Fuller taught her the rudiments and Anne Sullivan Macy carried on the training through painstaking years.

Having made this explanation to the vaudeville audience, Mrs. Macy turned to Miss Keller who throughout the narrative had been seated silently in view of the audience. The teacher took Helen's hand and demonstrated how she "spoke" into it. Then Helen "looked" out over the audience. Her face became radiant, her lips moved, and the people heard her say in measured, understandable tones, "I am not dumb now."

The audience barraged her with questions which Mrs. Macy quickly transmitted to her: "How old are you? Can you tell time without your raised watch? Can you remember hands that you touch, the way people remember faces? Do you enjoy traveling? Would you like to get married?"

Her sense of humor as she answered her inquisitors brought laughter and applause, but her plea for the blind and deaf, to which she always returned, quieted them with a reflection upon their duty to the handicapped and filled them with a new appreciation of the blessings of sight and sound.

My aunt's admiration for Helen Keller increased. "God," she maintained, "is nearer and more real to her than He is to most of us."

3.

These youthful remembrances matured and crystallized when I saw Helen Keller in Rochester, Minnesota, in October, 1938. She was appearing at a local school and I had come from a nearby college where I was teaching.

The setting could not have been more dramatic, the legend could not have been made more real, for she was speaking to pupils at the Central School, pupils of the age I had been when I first heard of her. They were becoming, as I had become in those days, a connecting link in her influence upon the world.

She was as I had imagined her to be, only that now her hair was gray. But she was strong and vigorous and inspiringly self-assured. Her voice, soft and toneless, at times so indistinct that we held our breath to catch her words, was also as I had imagined it. Her vivid and expressive hands, the light in her eyes, her smiling face—I felt I had seen all this before. But the inner radiance, the "presence" that was mystical—that I had never seen.

It was a transforming presence, as though God were native to her heart and as though there had never been a scene or a secret that He had hidden from her. During that first moment I could not believe that she was actually blind and deaf.

"Good morning, boys and girls," was her greeting. "I am happy to be with you if only for a little while. As my beloved teacher made my life bright and sweet, so shall your teachers blaze fresh trails for you for accomplishments and beauty of living."

And as I heard her speak and as those around me—superintendent, teachers, and pupils—felt as unashamed as I of the emotion that caught at our hearts, I thought again of what this American immortal embodies in her life.

I said to myself that Fate has willed that she should belong to a different world, a dark and silent world, but that in it she heard a voice, and the voice said, "Rise up and magnify the Lord."

I saw myself in her place and my youthful thoughts and remembrances rushed back upon me, causing me to wonder what I would do if I were standing where she stood.

I heard her say to the pupils, "If you try to do something good every day to someone else, you will keep happy and find life great and beautiful." And I saw the children look at her with wonder and awe.

I thought about the things I worry over and the things that distress me and the matters that upset me and tested my temper and I was moved with quietude as I saw her smile. I remembered how someone told me that "God is nearer and more real to her" and that is how it seemed to me now.

I knew that she was the last person who would want to be idealized and the first who would want to shatter the legends and the deification which some have tried to impose upon her, and yet I felt that she had been placed here on earth for a special purpose.

And I felt as I had seldom felt before—that the good life must be earnestly sought and that whosoever seeks, finds. I suddenly knew that the most enduring moments are those of the inner vision and the inner search.

I was presented to her, as most of us were that day, and I felt that this was a moment I would never forget. Sentimentally I paraphrased a familiar religious expression, "I saw her once, she touched my hand, then passed beyond my ken. I saw her once, but this I know, that as I was I shall not be again."

She spoke to a special group that day, a class of some thirty boys and girls who were totally or partially deaf. They sat at their desks, hands folded, eyes bright with excitement as their lovely visitor addressed them as, "Members of the silent lands" and assured them that their teachers were helping them to meet their destiny "side by side."

One of the youngest of the boys was asked by the director of the Oral school to write their guest's name on the blackboard. He got up eagerly, hurried to the board and wrote, "Helen Cellor." Quickly he corrected it, but not without Miss Keller catching, somehow, the humor of the affair. Then she took the boy and clasped him in her arms.

When Superintendent G. H. Sandberg thanked her for appearing, he unashamedly brushed back his tears. Later he told me that seeing Helen Keller had been for him a spiritual experience. All of us who left the classrooms felt that way and knew that our lives had been softened and enriched.

Her companion was Miss Polly Thomson, who stood in the place of Anne Sullivan Macy who had died in 1936. Years earlier Miss Keller had written, "I have frequently been asked what I should do without her. I smile and answer cheerfully, 'God sent her, and if He takes her, His love will fill the void, but it terrifies me to face the thought that this question brings to mind. I should be blind and deaf in very truth if she were gone away.' "

God gave her Polly Thomson of Glasgow, Scotland. She had been associated with the Keller household since 1914, the year Helen's mother had died. She came to "fill the void" and fill it well with a devotion worthy of the former "guardian angel."

There is an aura and a presence that one sees and feels in Helen Keller. Sensing it, George Bernard Shaw remarked, "Would that all Americans could see as well as you." Touched by it, sculptor Jo Davidson said, "We are all good when we are with you." Deeply aware of it, psychologist William James told her, "The sum of it is that you are a blessing." Dwight D. Eisenhower was moved to tears at his meeting with her, but he smiled for her so that she might "see" with her fingertips the man as she intuitively knew him to be.

There is an aura and it has caused people throughout the world to say, "She is a light and a hope."

I found evidences of it during a recent mission in India. Frequently when I asked, "Whom do you consider our greatest living American?" the answer was, "Helen Keller."

Mother India took her to its heart. Dr. M. Modi, the renowned eye specialist, assured me that no one had ever inspired such courage among India's blind. The government of New Delhi invited her to advise Indian institutions on the care of the handicapped. Rajendra Prasad, the first president of India, pressed a pebble from Mt. Everest into her hand and heard her say, "To think that I am holding Everest which looks down on all the world!"

There is something else she holds: the presence of the Christ as the personification of love in the human heart. It is not the sentimentality or the emotionalism found in Therese Neumann. It is not love objectified, but love employed in service. It is at once an outgoing and an incoming love, not as the fulfillment of desire, but love as duty. And even more, duty as a divine command, a mystical experience. That is what she has found in Him. She has found in Him the Mystical Presence, and in this union with Him, she is united with all living things, is inspired to live in two worlds at once, and is given an almost unerring spiritual sense to distinguish between the apparent and the real.

4.

Let me tell you how her path crossed the path of the Man from Nazareth and let us meet some of the people who guided her along the way.

The spiritual revelation began with the influence of Anne Sullivan. In fact, we can discover an analogy between the circumstances of this relationship and the awakening that takes place in many persons during their spiritual quest. For there are those of us who live in spiritual darkness until a teacher comes, a teacher who helps us discover the "water of life" and defines for us the association between reality and symbol.

There is an analogy here and no one would understand it better than Helen Keller herself. She knows what is meant by a leap in the dark from thoughts to things. She learned this early in life—at the pump-house. The reality of water and the word "water" ignited something in her spirit; it bridged the gap between the abstract expression and the object, and sent a momentary spiritual flash vibrating between her consciousness and divine consciousness. Until that moment her life had been a kind of somnambulistic wandering in the jungle of unrelated experiences. Having made the leap, the true meaning of life lay clearly in her path.

The *name* of God came into her life through her fingertips, as did most other words. She ran across it one day on the raised type when she was eight years old. She found God in raised print and began to perceive—aided by the ever-patient wise counsel of her teacher—that the mind can be independent of physical limitations. She realized she could take fancy flights. She could make believe she was not confined by space and time. She could even "see" with an inner vision.

Dreams played their part in this. The more she learned, the more vivid became her dreams. Sometimes she even felt that in her dreaming she was no longer blind and deaf. These were the "rare and beautiful moments," and once she asked herself, "What if in my waking hours a sound *should* ring through the silent halls of my hearing? What if a ray of light *should* flash through the darkened chambers of my soul? What would happen? Would the bow-and-string tension of life snap? Would the heart, overweighted with sudden joy, stop beating for the very excess of happiness?"

She never ceased looking for miracles, but she was never agonized by the want of them. The greatest miracle was the advent of her teacher, the coming of the presence.

Now, here was G-O-D in raised type. Here was the feeling of a connection between the freedom of her spirit and the spirit of God. Here were her dreams. All of this strengthened a conviction that some superhuman and intelligent Power had made the earth and life and all the many things beyond the skills of man.

God and this power could indeed be one, just as the word "water" had been one with the cool stream that flowed over her hand.

Water had many worlds in which it lived: the cup, the subterranean well, the rivers, the oceans, and the rain. And God had many worlds in which He lived. She had felt Him in the purr of a cat and in the warmth and the beating heart of a dog she loved. She had found Him in the wings of a bird. Taught by her teacher to be unafraid, she had patted and stroked animals in the zoo, had shaken hands with a bear, had permitted a snake to coil itself around her neck. All these were worlds. God's worlds.

Sometimes in moments of despair at her seemingly slow progress to learn, she had buried her tear-stained face in the grass and had felt the earth like a comforting mother beneath her. This, too, was a world. And there was the world of odors to which she was extremely sensitive. The flowered paths, the blossoming orchards, the trees and vines and shrubs presented a scented world through which she could find her way and in which there were many telltale signs of the soul of God. Such were her earliest mystical musings.

She had received no pre-knowledge of God other than from this inner, spiritual source. She harbored no learned prejudice about Him, no indoctrination, no religious conditioning such as most children have by the time they are eight. She had heard no one insist that God belongs to this group or that, or that He must be reached by any one specific path. She was alone among the innocent, as few have been. Yet the questions she asked were our questions, "Who has seen God? Where was my soul before I was born? Where does my soul go when I die?"

One morning she brought a handful of violets to Miss Sullivan. The teacher spelled into her hand, "I love Helen."

"What is love?" Helen wanted to know.

"It is here," said Anne Sullivan, placing Helen's hand upon her heart.

"Is love the sweetness of flowers? Is love the warm sun shining?"

"Love," she was told, "is something like the clouds that were in the sky before the sun came out. You cannot touch the clouds, but you feel the rain and know how glad the flowers and the thirsty earth are to have it after a hot day. You cannot touch love either, but you feel the sweetness that it pours into everything."

This was the beginning of a relationship between God and Love. God, too, could not be touched, could not be fully explained. He could only be felt—as love is felt. He could only be experienced, as love is experienced, mystically.

At about this time a renowned American cleric, a man ahead of the rigid orthodoxy of his day, became Helen's devoted friend. He was Phillips Brooks, rector of Boston's Trinity Church and, later, bishop of the Episcopal diocese of Massachusetts. First and foremost he was a lover of Christ. His lectures on "The Influence of Jesus" had brought him world acclaim. His Christmas hymn, "O Little Town of Bethlehem," had made him the friend of children everywhere.

It was he who explained to Helen Keller the personification of God's love in Jesus and it was he who literally took her by the hand and led her into the path of the mystical Jesus.

"You know, Helen," he told her in substance, "love is

at the soul of everything and Jesus is at the soul of love. The more we love, the closer we live to Him. Now, there are many good people in the world, but that does not mean that they are exempt from suffering. Jesus suffered more than anyone, and yet He was the best person and, I am sure, the happiest person that the world has ever seen. Why? Because His heart was full of the love of God. And so He loved men Himself, and though they were very cruel to Him and at last killed Him, He was willing to die because He loved us. And, Helen, He loves men still, and He loves us, and He tells us that we may love Him. Love is everything. And if anyone should ever ask you, or if you ask yourself what God is, answer: God is love.' "

Her admiration for Phillips Brooks was very great and so her mortal path crossed the inevitable path of the Divine. She made a disposition of Jesus and He became for her the mystical embodiment of love and duty beyond the comprehension of mortal man. We can understand Helen Keller only in the light of this experience. Jesus, walking faithfully despite suffering, serving God in selfless love, put her under orders to do her part in leaving her generation and her world a little better than she found it.

That is why she insisted upon getting an education, graduating from Radcliffe College with honors, and winning a degree of Doctor of Laws from both Glasgow University in Scotland and Witwatersrand University in Johannesburg, South Africa. That is why she took to the vaudeville stage, the lecture platform, the Chautauqua tent, the town hall, and the schoolroom, imparting courage and hope and urging help for the handicapped long before we were ever stirred by a feeling that they should be permitted to find their place.

That is why, while we moved in the light making our lives comfortable and secure, she moved about in the dark soliciting help for the unfortunate, motivated by the mystical concept that since God's love is universal and just, it must be manifested in all people everywhere.

There was a universality about her faith, too, that attracted me to her philosophy. Bishop Brooks, she made clear, had taught her no special creed or dogma. He had not insisted that she unite with his church or with any church. He had been content to impress upon her mind the two greatest commandments: love of God and love for man. According to the Boston cleric, Christianity could best be defined as the re-enactment of the life of Christ in the life of each individual.

An ardent reader of William James, Helen Keller was also influenced by his view that religion cannot be confined to any one institutionalized expression. William Blake gave her another insight into the universality and mysticism of faith when he spoke of his wish to "open the Eternal Worlds, to open the immortal eyes of man inwards into the Worlds of thought, into Eternity. . . ." The philosophy of René Descartes fixed her mind on the absolute by his memorable phrase, "I think, therefore I am."

Walt Whitman, her favorite poet, helped to shape her belief in the oneness of religion and people through his lines:

It seems to me there are other men in other lands, yearning and thoughtful;
And it seems to me if I could know those men, I should become attached to them, as I do to men in my own lands;
Oh, I know we should be brethren and lovers,
I know I should be happy with them.

And that is how she felt, too.

5.

The book which influenced her most was the Bible and the mind which helped most in her understanding of its hidden meaning was the mind of Emanuel Swedenborg.

As early as 1928 she paid her tribute to him when she wrote, "I plunge my hands deep into my large Braille volumes containing Swedenborg's teachings, and withdraw them full of the secrets of the spiritual world."

Emanuel Swedenborg had for many years meant nothing more to me than a name on the outer fringe of the institutionalized church. He was lodged in my memory as a hazy figure, as legendary as Helen Keller herself. But now my search for the basis of her belief led me straight to this Swedish seer.

There were others who had praised him. Franklin D. Roosevelt said, "The career of Emanuel Swedenborg emphasizes in a striking way the triumph of the spiritual over the material, and the vitality and inspiration of his message find eloquent witness in the hearts of his disciples today."

John Haynes Holmes called him a "colossal genius." Joseph Fort Newton declared that there had never been so great a mind or so humble a heart. Edwin Markham referred to him as "one of the greatest intellects that has ever appeared on this planet." James Moffatt insisted that Swedenborg was a prophet who saw visions of another world and whose revelations could be confirmed by Scripture.

He was the genius of geniuses: an eminent psychologist, linguist, hydrographer, mineralogist, cosmologist, and aeronautical engineer of the eighteenth century. His most important contribution was spiritual.

Helen Keller's *My Religion* prompted me to try to comprehend Swedenborg. I acquired his many books and tried to find my way, particularly through the most important of these, the *Arcana Coelestia.* It was not easy. I interviewed Swedenborgians, members of what is called the New Church, but became ever more enmeshed in the maze of esoteric teachings. Swedenborg, the Stockholm sage, was, I feared, beyond my grasp. But I always came back to Helen Keller. She testified,

"His message has traveled like light side by side with the new science, the new freedom, and the new society. . . . As I wander through the dark, encountering difficulties, I am aware of encouraging voices that murmur from the spirit realm. I sense a holy passion pouring down from the springs of Infinity. I thrill to music that beats with the pulses of God. Bound to suns and planets by invisible cords, I feel the flame of eternity in my soul. Here, in the midst of the everyday air, I sense the truth of ethereal rains. I am conscious of the splendour that binds all things of earth to all things of heaven. Immured by silence and by darkness, I possess the light which shall give me vision a thousandfold when death sets me free."

When I read and reread these words, when I closed my eyes and thought of Helen Keller and her faith, when I saw the light of her philosophy even as I had felt the light of her presence, I knew what was at the heart of it: the mystical belief (emphasized by Swedenborg) that Jesus—in whom God is—is also in Humanity. And not in Humanity only but in angels and spirits and in all that lives in this world and every other world as well. Jesus had come again, not in a physical second coming, but in spirit and in truth.

So thinking, it became clear that when we serve and help others, we are serving Him. When we love others we are loving Him. When we truly find ourselves, we are finding Him. And there was no doubt in my mind that when Helen Keller walked in the world she was walking with Him.

I could now understand why Swedenborg would appeal especially to her. He was neither superficial nor apparent. He was constantly relating the real and the unseen to the apparent and the seen. He was always pushing back our world or, rather, intertwining our world with other worlds, even as the girl Helen Keller had done with the many worlds of God. Somehow, she had been prepared for this Christian mysticism before her fingertips ever touched the name of God. Who could understand better than she that there *must* be many worlds, particularly a world of darkness and a world of light? Who could know better than she that God's world knew neither light nor darkness? And who had approached the Master in humanity more tenderly than she?

Her Bible took on new and deeper meaning when she read it according to Swedenborg's teaching. He taught that the Word of God had been dictated by God and inspired in every letter and word, and that besides its literal sense adapted to men, it contained also a spiritual sense adapted to angels. He believed, and Hellen Keller believed, that these senses are connected with each other by the law of harmony or *correspondences.* Swedenborg claimed that by way of these correspondences he had penetrated not only the hidden meaning of Scripture, but the hidden meaning of all life. He had communed with angels and he was at home in both the natural and the spiritual world.

He taught that the whole of God was present in Christ. God took upon Himself human form and dwelt among men. This was similar to other orthodox teachings, but Swedenborg found its deepest meaning. He taught that the Trinity consisted not only of Father, Son, and Holy Spirit, but also of an "innermost essence." The essence of the Father, he explained, is Love. The essence of the Son is Wisdom. The essence of the Holy Sipirt is the Divine Operation of heavenly power. This "essence" is again discoverable in man where it resides as soul, body, and action. Thus, he maintained, man has communication with, and citizenship in, the unseen world.

Teachings of this nature, centering around the cardinal principle that Jesus is the sole and only God, building worlds within worlds, calling upon men to see the unseen, asking an end to the dissension among creeds, visualizing all churches as "gems in a King's Crown," and recognizing that eternity is already here, caused Helen Keller to declare, "One thing I know, that whereas I was blind, now I see!" She meant, of course, a spiritual insight and, like Swedenborg, she meant that she was in communication with the other worlds while living this mortal life.

Ever since her path crossed the path of Jesus, she saw Him everywhere at work. And she works, too, motivated by the mystical essence of love in the Father. Her lectures and fund-raising programs take her all over the world. She finds time to visit wounded veterans in American war hospitals and to work intensively for Europe's handicapped. From her Westport, Connecticut, home she assists in the work of numerous societies and institutions. During the depression she raised $1,000,000 for the American Foundation for the Blind, then donated to the Foundation the $5,000 award she received for her achievement. She played in a motion picture based on her life and as recently as 1956 co-operated in a new release, "Helen Keller In Her Story," in which Katharine Cornell is the narrator.

How does she do it?

"True Christian religion," she says "is full of stimuli for faith in our God-given powers and self-activity. . . . We should never surrender to misfortunes or circumstances or even to our faults hopelessly, passively—as if we were but carved images with our hands hanging down, waiting for God's grace to put us into motion. We should give no quarter to spiritual slavery. We should take the initiative, look into ourselves fearlessly, search out new ideas of what to do, and ways to develop our will power. Then God will give us enough light and love for all our needs."

She met the Man from Nazareth and saw in Him the Mystical Presence.

Had she lived at the time of Jesus she would have walked with Him through the valleys no less than upon the mountain heights. She, more than anyone, would not have hesitated to have gone with Him steadfastly along the way of the Cross and upward to that hill.

She would have said to those who flocked to Him out of curiosity or want that the true discovery of Him is in one's heart. She would have said that His identity with God is the first doctrine and that man's identity with Him is the first qualification of discipleship. Finding Christ means, for her, the forgetting of one's own selfish wants and needs. It means conquering worries and triumphing over the strains of life and sacrificing oneself for the sake of the soul one is helping.

She would have told those who despaired of suffering and longed for deliverance and who wondered about the meaning of faith, "If you can enjoy the sun and flowers where there is nothing except darkness and silence, you have proved the mystic sense."

Had she lived in Jesus' time she would have seen that

which even the disciples failed to see, God Himself walking among them.

She would have reminded Thomas that there is always a spiritual meaning within the literal and she might have said to him, "Close your eyes and look upon Him with your inner vision. Then you will no longer doubt." And to Peter, "Life is changed not from without, but from within." And to John, "Good and truth are received as good and truth by those who are good. But by the evil, good and truth are received as evil and falsehood." And to Judas Iscariot, "There is a mental hell into which people go who are self-confirmed lovers of evil, and who wilfully deny God in their heart." To all of the disciples she might conceivably have put the question, "Why do you dispute among yourselves as to who should be greatest in His Kingdom? You misinterpret His work of love as a plan of conquest and personal glory."

These were some of her convictions; this was her faith in which she believed with profound certainty. The mystical Christ whom she met triumphantly in the dark corridors of her pilgrimage became the light of her life. His spirit forms her credo and in the annals of American religious thought, it is difficult to find a more majestic and inspiring *I Believe*. She has recorded it with unearthly beauty and feeling in her book *Midstream*:

"I believe that we can live on earth according to the teachings of Jesus, and that the greatest happiness will come to the world when man obeys His Commandment, 'Love ye one another.'

"I believe that every question between man and man is

a religious question, and that every social wrong is a moral wrong.

"I believe that we can live on earth according to fulfillment of God's will, and that when the will of God is done on earth as it is done in heaven, every man will love his fellow men, and act toward them as he desires they should act toward him. I believe that the welfare of each is bound up in the welfare of all.

"I believe that life is given us so we may grow in love, and I believe that God is in me as the sun is in the colour and fragrance of a flower—the Light in my darkness, the Voice in my silence.

"I believe that only in broken gleams has the Sun of Truth yet shone upon men. I believe that love will finally establish the Kingdom of God on earth, and that the Cornerstones of that Kingdom will be Liberty, Truth, Brotherhood and Service.

"I believe that no good shall be lost, and that all man has willed or hoped or dreamed of good shall exist forever.

"I believe in the immortality of the soul because I have within me immortal longings. I believe that the state we enter after death is wrought of our own motives, thoughts, and deeds. I believe that in the life to come I shall have the senses I have not had here, and that my home there will be beautiful with colour, music, and speech of flowers and faces I love.

"Without this faith there would be little meaning in my life. I should be 'a mere pillare of darkness in the dark.' Observers in the full enjoyment of their bodily senses pity me, but it is because they do not see the golden chamber in my life where I dwell delighted; for, dark as my path may seem to them, I carry a magic light in my heart. Faith, the spiritual strong searchlight, illumines the way, and although sinister doubts lurk in the shadow, I walk unafraid toward the Enchanted Wood where the foliage is always green, where joy abides, where nightingales nest and sing, and where life and death are one in the Presence of the Lord."

Her path crossed the path of the Man from Nazareth and she made of Him a Mystical Presence. She has that kind of a mind—and heart.

5.

POPE PIUS XII

Then there was Pope Pius XII. The first time I saw him was at the consistory when seventeen new cardinals got their red hats in a most imposing ceremony in the largest and richest church in the world.

It was a January day in 1953. I was jammed inside St. Peter's Basilica, a link in a tangled chain of humanity that had packed the holy precincts since early dawn. Forty thousand people were pressed in such close bodily contact that a woman near me fainted and could not fall. An armed guard broke a path for a nurse and the unfortunate one was eventually taken outside.

A monk clung to the slippery leg of a bronze statue so that he was head and shoulders above the crowd. Parish priests, squeezed by the throng, complacently read their offices. A pamphleteer, daring to show the Communist side of things, handed out tracts on Vishinsky and Stepanic. There was a young mother who protectingly clutched her child in her arms, and there was also an old woman who kept chanting, "*Viva il Papa,*" under her breath. And there were three men and two women who balanced themselves on a strip of marble wainscoting not more than two-inches wide.

Referring to this group, an American soldier, who envied them their perch, turned to me and said, "They can't hold out much longer."

"Don't kid yourself," another American voice cut in. "They're Germans. They've been there since seven o'clock."

It was now nine. I closed my eyes and tried to catch a familiar word out of the jangled voices. The drone of many languages was like a modern Pentecost. The world had come to Rome for this consistory.

Thousands had not gotten through St. Peter's lofty doors. They were planted like a living forest out in Vatican Square. They had come early in the morning, hopeful that some passes might be available. Failing in this, they had stayed to watch the amazing paradox: church dignitaries, dressed as if they had just stepped out of a Michelangelo fresco, arriving in sleek, modern limousines; nuns, attired in habits styled in the Middle Ages, coming by taxi; friars, robed as those in the days of Cortez, escorted by traffic police.

For weeks the Vatican palaces had been over-run. The eleven thousand rooms in this fairyland of faith were booked solid by the princes and statesmen of Mother Church. For days we lowly outsiders—travelers and seekers and newsmen and common garden variety of Christians—had moved with proper awe through the Treasure Room and the Sistine Chapel and the Chiaramonti Museum, trying to comprehend the meaning and the value of statues, busts, paintings, sarcophagi, vestments, mitres, rings, relics, reliquaries, jewels and all other existing monuments of precious ancient art.

We had been dazzled by the *Illuminati* in the Vatican Library which holds the world's most prized collections.

We had climbed the various roof levels and the dome of St. Peter's, outside, to gaze over the Eternal City to see how many of Rome's 365 churches we could spot. We had climbed it inside to prove that the guide book was right when it said, "The interior dome is 390 feet high and if you look down over the rail, one feels really giddy."

At nine twenty-five the tension in the tangled chain of humanity increased. The monk who dangled from the statue's leg swung part way around. The group of Germans on the ledge looked victorious as if now they knew they could hold out until the final moment. The young mother holding her child pressed forward, closer to the roped-off aisle. The old woman looked up with tired eyes. Her words were now a question, "*Viva il Papa*?" She was asking, "Is he coming? Can you see anything? Is this the great moment?" Then the tension passed and the unintelligible drone of many languages again resumed.

At nine-thirty, high in a niche near the Porta Sancta, which is opened once every twenty-five years, a group of sentries raised silver trumpets to their lips. The fanfare resounded through the marble halls like a shrill voice out of heaven. The bronze door was moving. Myriads of lights sprang into life around us and overhead to form a kind of Milky Way across St. Peter's vaulted sky.

Now the door was open. Towering Swiss guards with plumed hats and breeches and vests of yellow and red marched in as if out of the pages of an ancient legend. Down the roped-off aisles they came, boots clopping down sharply on the marble floor, heads up and halberds flashing.

Behind them, against a background of soldiers, archbishops, procurators, chaplains, monks, and priests, came a moving throne, high and mighty, borne on the shoulders of twelve stalwart men; and on the throne a frail and slender figure sat.

"*Viva il Papa!*" Thousands of voices screamed the greeting. The crowd threw kisses, waved flags and banners, wept, cheered, and dropped to their knees inside the shoving, writhing mass.

"*Viva il Papa!*"

A thin, silken vestment of shimmering white covered his fragile body. Over this was draped a red mantle trimmed in gold, and the jeweled tiara on his head seized the light of the electric stars and cast it down on us who welcomed him. He was a king, the emperor of Vatican State, whose scepter was a crucifix. His attendants, carrying fans of ostrich feathers on long sticks, bore themselves as if honoring a Solomon. His court surrounded him, and in his holy train came cardinals resplendent in their flowing scarlet robes and ermine capes.

"*Viva il Papa!*"

The man on the throne made the sign of the cross over and over, leaned slightly forward, turned to left and right as he was borne toward the high altar which rises over the tomb of St. Peter. Lights were added to lights along his path through the cheering crowds. Cathedral guards who had taken their places near the ropes joined hands to form a human wall and hold back the throngs as the holy cavalcade marched by.

Far down the aisle, on an elevated, glassed-in platform six-hundred feet away, the Sistine choir began to sing. From where I stood the singers looked like marionettes, but the music was that of angelic voices, silencing the most noisy of the demonstrators.

Il Papa had now reached Peter's tomb where the ninety-five lamps burn day and night. Here stood the mighty papal chair, somewhat dwarfed by the four bronze pilasters which rise high above the sixteen-foot statues and serve to form the four chapels. Here *il Papa* took his place amidst the most precious relics of Mother Church. Most of us knew the mystery and the magic of this holy place. Not only was the body of St. Peter interred beneath this hallowed spot, but each of the four chapels held an equally momentous object for veneration: the actual head of St. Andrew; the veil of Veronica; a part of the true Cross; the lance with which one of the soldiers pierced the body of our Lord. Here the Pope sat down while the attendants with the ostrich fans stood near him on either side.

The old woman's words were a whisper, "*Viva il Papa?*"

Had she seen him? No. She was too diminutive and much too old for that. She only knew that he had passed by. Not even his shadow had fallen on her. She could not have touched the outermost hem of his garment, but she had had her say, "*Viva il Papa!* Long live the Pope!"

All around me people had their backs turned to the pontifical ceremony and were holding small reflectors high above their heads. In this way an arm's length extension was given to their vision even though the position was awkward. It must have been like watching the action through a rear-view mirror. Several children sat gleefully on the shoulders of grownups, and by this time the legs and laps and arms of the huge statues were nested with eager onlookers.

A guard was pushing his way through the excited crowd.

"Signor!" I called. "I have a special ticket. Can you get me closer to the ceremony?"

He paused to look me over. I handed him an American dollar.

He said, "Follow me."

With many a "Pardon me!" and "Make way, if you please!" he got me through the human walls and up on one of the temporary bleachers. A thousand or more, who also held red cards marked *Anticamera Pontificia,* were already seated on this precarious backless rigging. I squeezed in, close enough now to hear the chant of the ceremonial Latin as the mighty princes of Mother Church were publicly installed.

Pope Pius XII sat in the papal chair, seven steps above the level of the marble floor. He looked like a china figure, fragile and white, but a power emanated from him; a power spiritual and unquestioned, evidenced in the slightest movement of his hand or nod of his mitered head. One by one the incumbent cardinals brought the scarlet clad candidates from the chapel. One by one they climbed the seven steps and knelt to kiss their Prince's hand. Then, in turn, the Pontifical Master of Ceremonies dramatically raised the *galero*, the broad-brimmed red hat, over the head of each kneeling dignitary and intoned the blessing in a cavernous voice:

In praise of Almighty God and as an ornament
Of the Holy Apostolic See,
Receive now the red hat,
Distinctive of the Cardinal's dignity;
It signifies that you must show yourself
Intrepid even unto shedding your blood,
For the exaltation of the Holy Faith——
For the peace of the Christian people——
And for the growth and glory of the Roman Church.
In the name of the Father,
The Son, and the Holy Ghost.
Amen.

The slender, exquisite figure, now wearing a red beret instead of a miter, stooped down and kissed both cheeks of each newly installed apostle of the "one and only Church of Christ." And while this was repeated, seventeen times, my eyes traveled to the other silent players in this ecclesiastical drama: the emissaries, the apostolic nuncios, the archbishops, bishops, priests. They all stood lost in worship, trance-like, under the spell of the ascetic figure who was, for them, earth's greatest mortal.

My Protestant mind asked the inevitable question, How shall one justify this worshipful adoration in the light of Him who never wished to be a king, never desired earthly pomp and power and adulation? How can the uncounted wealth of Mother Church be reconciled with His kingdom that was not of this world?

Even more tantalizing was another question: What kind of man is this who, in every act and movement, seems a king? What would he be like if one could meet him privately? Pope Pius XII. This man, who for years had been in the public eye as Papal Nuncio to Germany in World War I, as Secretary of the Vatican State, as Papal Legate to Eucharistic Congresses in many parts of the World—what was he really like?

A thought came to me as the *galeros* were lifted up and as the thousands from every nation around me made the eternal sign of the cross: would I kiss the Pope's ring if he granted me an audience? It was an amusing conjecture, and into my imaginings came my old preacher uncle, of stern and bearded face, who, when he walked down the street past the Catholic Church back home, crossed to the other side; an aunt who was convinced an arsenal was hidden behind those bronze-hinged doors; an uncle who used to read the *Menace*; a mother whose moment of greatest concern was when I thought I was in love with a Catholic girl; and friends who openly got into the fray to keep Roosevelt from sending a personal representative to the Vatican. Would I kiss the Pope's ring?

Down went another *galero*. This time on an American, His most Reverend Excellency, James Francis McIntyre, of California.

. . . . intrepid even unto shedding your blood,
For the exaltation of the Holy Faith——
For the peace of the Christian people——
And for the growth and glory of the Roman Church. . . .

The Helvetian guards stood in the roped-off aisle, prepared to escort St. Peter's successor back through the marble path. The throne was lifted up amid a blaze of song and glory. Tiara once more on head, smiling upon the kneeling and cheering subjects, the Pope was transported in a procession more colorful by far than any procession that ever entered or emerged from Jerusalem. Already an overpowering shout exploded outside and cries drowned out the music as acres of people, who had been standing for four hours in the damp and dreary cold, demanded that he appear to them on the open loggia of St. Peter's. He would not disappoint them. He never did. Pope Pius XII knew and loved his people.

An hour later, released from the human chain that had bound me, I walked through St. Peter's Square and down the Via Della Conciliazione where hawkers and sidewalk concessions scandalized my Protestant mind by raffling off their holy wares. Nonetheless, I bought a few rosaries for friends and a missal for myself and watched the passing parade here, near the headquarters of what Catholics refer to as, "the Corporation Christ founded for the saving of souls." Bells were ringing and banners were flying as if to assure me that the grant for this corporation had been legally transferred from the Twelve Apostles and Jesus to the seventy cardinals and the Pope, and that, as Catholics often said, "There is no heaven for us outside the Catholic Church." Dislike this, if you wish, was their attitude; resent it if you will—what difference does it make? Truth is truth, they seemed to say, and if you find Rome too "popish" what can you do about that? If it were not Rome, it would have to be Paris or Vienna or Washington. The Holy Father must live somewhere.

2.

That evening, when I got back to my hotel, the clerk handed me a note. "You will receive," it advised, "an invitation for a special audience with Pope Pius XII for Thursday morning at eleven o'clock. I am very happy that this is to be your privilege and hope you can make it." The note was signed James Naughton, S. J.

Months earlier in the American Midwest, in Omaha, I had spoken at a meeting of the Nebraska State Educational Association. My topic, dealing with Protestant-Catholic relations, had enabled me to suggest the possibility of a rapprochement between Christianity's divided house and to voice a hope of ultimate reunion at some distant day. I said that Protestantism, always a prophetic faith, was becoming more priestly, and that priestly Catholicism was tending to become more prophetic. It was my thought that divided Christendom represented not parallel lines which would meet only in infinity, but converging lines which at some not too distant day might bring ecumenical Protestantism and Catholicism to a realization of the Messianic prayer "that they may be one."

During the question period on that occasion a man

had risen quickly to his feet. He was a benign, patriarchal figure with graying hair. He was a priest, the only one in the crowded hall. A hush fell over everyone just then, as, with splendid poise, he addressed himself to the chairman of the meeting.

"I do not have a question," he began. "I have a statement. I want to say that what our speaker has presented as a trend and as a hope is exactly what I have been telling my people and my students for some time. I want only to heartily endorse what has been said."

Then he sat down. His words and his voice rested upon us like a benediction, and when he came to talk to me later I was doubly assured of his sincerity. It might be that he thought in terms of everyone some day becoming a Catholic, but for a little while we stood together united in a spiritual awareness that recognized Something beyond denominational lines.

"Let me know if I can ever be of service to you," he said.

"You can do something for me right now," I told him. "I plan to be in Rome at the time of the consistory and if you could make some connection for me so that I might have a guide to take me off the beaten paths, that would be fine."

"I'll be happy to do that," he promised.

A few days later this Omaha priest and educator, the Reverend Francis Bowdern, S. J., sent me two letters of introduction. One was in Latin and the other an English translation: "Permit me to introduce my very dear friend

——for many years he has been making intimate studies of religions other than his own——he is eager to see at close range whatever will increase his understanding of our faith. I beg you to give him every assistance."

This generous recommendation had been my pass-key in many European cities where I interviewed Catholic dignitaries, and in Rome it led the way to Father James Naughton in the office of the Jesuit General.

Naughton, an American in his forties, was one of those men who unconsciously prove that a highly trained, scientific mind can co-exist with humility. He loved the Church and lived with God. Any Protestant would have concluded that he was a mixture of wisdom and naïveté when it came to religion, and every Protestant would have envied him his faith and his security in what he believed.

I once asked him about his reaction to the dogma of the Assumption, the doctrine which holds that the Virgin Mary entered heaven, body and soul, by the power of God. This concept, which had been held by the Church for several centuries, was officially established as a dogma by Pope Pius XII in 1950.

"What do I think of it?" Naughton replied with quiet rapture. "I not only believe and accept it, but to me it figures in one of my most thrilling remembrances. I'll never forget the day the Holy Father announced it. St. Peter's Square was packed solid with perhaps half a million people. This was the first time Pope Pius XII had ever made a statement on doctrine from outside St.

Peter's itself. The day was one of those wonderful August days, and the weather itself seemed to be co-operating for the glory of the event. The Holy Father in tiara and mantle was carried out on his gestatorial chair. All the people fell to their knees. The bells, which had been ringing, suddenly stopped. The Holy Father began to read slowly and thoughtfully, almost a bit nervously. You see, we feel that this message is really the truth of God. If it were not the truth, God would not have let it be uttered. Here was a man speaking as the mouthpiece of God and if what he was saying was a lie, who knew but that he might have been struck dumb or dead before he got through. So the Holy Father read this pronouncement and when *Urbs et Orbis*—the city and the world—had heard it, there was a great triumphant uproar."

His voice thrilled as he continued. "I used to read in old church histories how people danced in the street, and now I was witnessing it. I was part of it. I was so happy I cried for joy. Perhaps this is because I have always loved Our Lady so very much. The streets of Rome took on the scene of love. Candles and torches were gotten ready for the evening celebration. From every window flags and tapestries began to wave. At every window a happy face appeared. That night St. Peter's was aglow with lights, and burning torches filled the streets. It was one of those never to be forgotten events. Those who try to explain the miracle of the Assumption by natural law cannot do so. Some skeptics say that if Mary ascended bodily to heaven she would have been burned to a crisp. That is all nonsense. God, who made natural law, can also set it aside."

Naughton became my friend and now he had proved his friendship by including me in this special audience with the champion of his faith.

3.

Surely the spirit of my old preacher uncle looked down on me the morning of my appointment. He was trying to part the many veils that hang between us and that other world. He was with me when a helmeted Swiss giant with halberd in hand stopped me ceremoniously at a bronze door.

I handed the guard my magic paper which bore the Vatican watermark and upon which SPECIALI UDIENZE was imposingly embossed. The guard looked at it. It was all he needed to impel him to click his heels and invite me in. In fact, whenever I met a man with a sword or gun, I disarmed him easily with this holy visa.

Through the marble corridors and up the *Scala Regis* I made my way. Jacob had his ladder, but it could have been no more resplendent than these imperishable stairs with their gleaming balustrades. Solomon had his Temple, but its magnificence could hardly have compared with that of the palace which encompassed this celestial heaven of the Holy See.

Everywhere guards stood stiffly at attention, but I was not questioned by them along this *via gloriae*. They evidently knew that since I had come this far I had a perfect right to go farther. Or, perhaps their sharp eyes already spied the paper in my hand. I came to an elevator and the attendant courteously examined my pass, then opened the elevator door. Several flights up he opened the door for me and I was greeted by papal gendarmes past whom I walked into a huge patio.

Here I was astonished to see several limousines parked and another rumbling over the cobblestones. Then a ramp leading down a steep incline solved the mystery of how these vehicles had gotten up here. I was inside a walled city, a fortress of some one hundred acres, the kingdom of Catholicism's supreme ruler. From the opposite side of the enclosure a chamberlain was beckoning.

He escorted me through several more corridors and rooms and finally presented me to the *bussolanti,* the audience courier, attired in formal dress with white tie. After checking the pronunciation of my name and home residence and asking in which language I wished to be addressed by His Holiness, he took me to a magnificent room with red damask-covered walls and equipped with a fireplace and several sumptuous chairs. Four grenadiers stood at ease with rifle butts resting on the thickly carpeted floor.

It was almost with relief that I realized I was not alone in this SPECIALI UDIENZE, for everything about the settings seemed designed to overawe the lone pilgrim to this holy shrine. At my left stood an Italian woman, elegant in long velvet gown and black lace mantilla. Her well cared for hands seemed never to have carried any heavier burden than her sparkling jewels and her dainty white lace handkerchief. Next to her was a French diplomat, an aloof and portly man, whose broad chest advantageously displayed a row of distinguished service medals.

At his side were four Dominican monks in the common brown habits of their order. They looked like men who might have come back from the dead, but I later learned they had been on a mission to China where they had suffered greatly. Now they waited, and wanted only the blessing of the Pope before going on to a new field of sacrifice and labor in Japan. Two of these men were German; two, Spanish. Next to them, hand in hand, stood a young Portuguese couple, newly-married, the bride still wearing her starched wedding veil. Somewhat apart from them was a small, sad-faced elderly woman dressed in deep mourning. A rosary dangled from her work worn hands.

A bell sounded in a corner of the room. At this signal the grenadiers whipped their rifles to their shoulders and stood at attention. In a moment an envoy crossed the room, portfolio in hand. As soon as he had gone, the guards again went back to an "at ease" position. Then the bell rang again and again they went through their routine, assuring the dignitary who now entered and crossed the room that he was being shown due military honors in the holy empire—an empire which boasts its own army, its own small corps of marines, and, since the sixteenth century, some two hundred Swiss troops who have sworn to protect and defend the Catholic Pontiff with their lives.

Now the *bussolanti* led us through a tapestried hall and finally to a door watched over by a towering sentry. We were invited to enter a relatively small, intimate chamber where a low throne stood against an inner wall. The severe silence of this room was happily broken by the tick of a grandfather clock.

We were asked to wait. The *bussolanti* went out through an adjoining door, and we stood in a semi-circle waiting. The clock showed eleven twenty-five.

I turned to the Italian woman and ventured to say, "He's late."

"Oh, do you not know," she whispered back. "He is still in conference with his Secretary of State."

I asked, "Are you tired of standing? There's a chair here."

"Tired?" she answered with a note of pain at my question. "I could stand here all day."

The rapture of her voice made me feel that I, too, ought to make every moment an adventure. The French diplomat cleared his throat and then took a deep and audible breath.

After ten minutes of waiting, the bell rang in the room from which we had come. I could hear the click of the rifles being snapped in the hands of the grenadiers. In a moment a door opened and a man in clerical attire, portfolio in hand, came out, gave us a quick glance and then made his exit. The woman at my side watched him until he had disappeared.

Turning to me, she said, "The Secretary of State."

The monks stood with bowed heads and folded hands.

In a moment the *bussolanti* returned. He looked over the group quickly, then drew himself erect as if urging us, by his example, to do the same. He rattled the sheaf of SPECIALI UDIENZE passes in his hand, then eased his collar a bit with a gesture that said, "I have gone through this hundreds of times. It is nothing new to me, but I don't want any slip-up this morning."

Even he was taken off guard by the almost magical entrance of a tall and regal figure. He came in so quickly and with such an element of surprise that before I knew what was happening, everyone had dropped to his knees —I, too. This might conceivably have been a planned entrance, even to the raised hand making the sign of the cross, but planned or not, it had the intended effect. We were already captives, and willing ones at that.

4.

The Pope uttered a Latin prayer; then we arose. He went to the woman in the velvet gown and conversed with her in Italian. He spoke to the diplomat in French; to two of the monks in German; and to the other two in Spanish. To the Portuguese couple he spoke Portuguese and Polish to the woman in mourning.

The *bussolanti* had, of course, informed him of the name and nationality of every person and this was the cue which started His Holiness on an unhurried, but businesslike conference with each. This multilingual talent should, of course, not have seemed so phenomenal to me in the light of the personal history of Pope Pius XII. He is considered one of the world's foremost masters of the art of "speaking in many tongues," and perhaps the greatest of the Church's philologists. On frequent occasions he has addressed assemblies in as many as eight languages.

Nonetheless, I was astonished and impressed and, during the thirty or more minutes taken up by his conversations in this audience chamber, I had a chance to register other impressions of the man.

He was dressed, not like a king, but like a monk. Today he was God's man and not the people's. In place of silken vestments and gold-woven mantle, he wore a plain white woolen habit with a small white cape over his frail shoulders. Instead of miter or tiara, his thin gray hair was covered by a small white skullcap. The only indication of the greatness of his station was the famous Fisherman's Ring on his right hand. It was this ring which each guest kissed while kneeling before him and pressing his hand. There was not the slightest hesitancy or question about this. From the decorated diplomat who whispered confidentially to the Mighty Pontiff, to the woman in mourning whose Rosary he blessed, the Holy Father graciously permitted each one to indulge in the highest mark of homage: the kissing of the ring. I watched and waited, and all the while every anti-Catholic voice of every one of my dear departed was saying, "Remember you're a Protestant!"

I remembered. But at the moment I did not quite know what to protest! I was here, by my own maneuvering, my own wishes and my own will; here, to form my own opinion of the slender but powerful man who now came around to me and looked at me studiously through shining spectacles. His eyes were jet black; his voice was warm and cordial as he greeted me in fluent English, launching immediately into a series of earnest questions about my life and work.

His interest was sincere, as if an audience of this kind afforded him his only chance to travel out among the children of the world. For surely, since becoming Pope of all the World, he has been a prisoner of the Vatican. His only occasional escape is to visit his summer palace, the Castel Gondolfo, some fourteen miles from the Eternal City.

I told him about various experiments in inter-religious relations in which I was engaged, and of my interest in better understanding among all Christian faiths. He was in full agreement. This led into a brief explanation on my part of the School of Religion at the University of Iowa where Catholic, Protestant, and Jewish professors are represented on the staff. When I told him that I was the Protestant teacher there he inquired about the courses and the curriculum and showed interest that such a program was possible in a state university.

His questions about the Midwest, its schools and its people, were a means of refreshing him on his knowledge of America, gained first-hand when he toured the United States in the early 1930s. At that time he was Papal Secretary of State. Notre Dame University conferred upon him the degree of Doctor of Letters and several other schools awarded him other honorary degrees. It was during his American visit that his acquaintance with President Roosevelt deepened into a friendship sealed by five years of warm correspondence and terminated only by F.D.R.'s sudden death. It was Roosevelt who, when Cardinal Pacelli became Pope in 1939, sent a personal representative to the Vatican despite the rising objection of Protestant opinion.

"Tell me something about your family," the Pope suggested.

Again I had the feeling that he was genuinely interested, not only as a matter of courtesy but because this "Roman of Rome," as he is often called, is first of all a good priest. And perhaps as Father of Princes and Kings, and Governor of all the World, as he is also called, he firmly believes that all who enter here, whatever their origin or station or color or speech, have equal rights as children of the God he serves.

"You are impressed with Rome?" he wanted to know.

I told him what had impressed me most, St. Paul's Outside the Walls; and what had thrilled me most, a visit to the catacombs with a friendly priest who seemed to relive the toils and fears of those who hid and worshiped there when the faith was young.

He smiled patiently and in understanding. For a moment any pretense, if any there had been, was put aside. He told me in a glance how grateful he was to hear, to *feel* would be more correct, that I felt this way about places and persons dear to the heart of Mother Church.

A man must believe, at least I did, that this intransigent leader has never lost his sentiment for the very smallest evidence of faithfulness on the part of his people. He seemed to be on the verge of exclaiming, "Yes, isn't it wonderful how my priests revere everything that is sacred to us?" He appeared to be delighted to have a reason for smiling instead of being the grave moderator of what is right and wrong.

Inevitably the conversation came around to the ceremony at which the cardinals had been elevated. He seemed pleased at my enthusiasm and divined that though I wasn't Catholic, I had a love for pageantry. Though the symbolism might be beyond me, the feeling and the emotional impact of the event would be long remembered.

Now he was holding out his hand to me. He pressed a small bronze medal into my palm.

"A remembrance of your audience," he was saying.

It was the size of a half dollar, a medallion bearing on one side an imprint of the Holy Family and on the other a profile around which was inscribed, *Pius XII Pontifex Maximus.*

As I raised my eyes, I found him still standing before me. His expression was one of quiet thoughtfulness, almost of yearning, as if he were saying, "I wonder what meaning that will have for you? I wonder where it will go with you, into what experiences and into what parts of this troubled world? Do carry it with you, won't you, as a remembrance of this day?"

It would be presumptuous for me to say that he is a lonely man or a man much misunderstood. I can only say that these were impressions which came to me during that moment. It is certainly no secret that among many non-Catholics it is believed that the Pope—any Pope—belongs in the legions of the anti-Christ. To me Pope Pius XII represented only the best, the lowliest, and the humblest.

And so thinking, I knelt down and touched my lips to the Fisherman's Ring.

I think I understand how a Catholic pilgrim must feel. For him, the Pope represents more than a tradition, more than a link in the apostolic chain. The Pope is, the Catholic believes, actually standing in the place of Christ. From this exalted station he sweeps away the age-old debate between Petros and Petra; puts aside the disputes of the apostles about who shall be greatest in the kingdom; removes from discussion such burning controversial topics as why some popes were wicked and cruel, how sinful men could still hold the "power of the keys," why Peter, himself, denied his Lord, and why the disciples, themselves, never recognized the primacy of Peter the Rock. Nothing matters to the Catholic who stands before the High Priest of Christendom beyond the fact that he has finally met the supreme mediator between himself and God.

To me the Pope was by no means Christ. He was by no means infallible. He was a sign, a figure of faith, no more, no less than any man who stands in the line of *spiritual* apostolic succession. But he stood there, dedicated heart and soul to what he believed. I remembered how my mother once kissed the hand of a missionary, not only because of what he was, but because of what he represented. He stood for those aspects of Christian service which life had never quite permitted *her* to perform in the foreign field. He was a symbol of a deep and unfilled yearning in her life. She had taken a different road. She sometimes felt she had not been obedient to the higher calling. She saw herself in the missionary, and so she kissed his hand.

I kissed the Fisherman's Ring. Then the Pope took hold of my right hand and lifted me up. He turned to say a final word to the Dominicans, after which he took his place in the center of our quiet circle and made the sign of the cross. We got down on our knees and he spoke a prayer. When I opened my eyes he had already walked from the room.

5.

As I made my way through the Hall of the Palatine Guards, down the grand staircases, and onward to the bronze door that opens to St. Peter's Square, I was again reminded of the power vested in this leader of the Roman Church. As king temporal and eternal, he is the undisputed authority for some 450,000,000 Christians. Four hundred thousand priests and followers of Holy Orders listen when he speaks. Seventy cardinals are bound to him by ties stronger than death and he has the power to "seal their lips." Whenever he speaks *ex cathedra* on the subject of faith and morals, every Catholic is expected to accept his pronouncement as infallible.

What makes this man so powerful? Is it the "sinister system" of scholarship that has been built upon the much debated passage, "Thou art Peter, the Rock?" Is it the insistence with which the Pope, any Pope, and the hierarchy he represents have claimed for themselves a solid monopoly on Christ's promise, "Whatsoever thou shalt loose on earth shall be loosed in heaven?" Does the basic, underlying network of clericalism produce his great official strength?—or is it the intricate political machinery that he commands? Does he actually hold some mystical or magical secret which gives him the right to custody of the keys of the kingdom? Is he powerful because he knows the hidden cabala that can get men out of purgatory and into heaven?

With this man it is none of these. Pius XII is what he is because his path crossed the path of the Man from Nazareth. The secret is no more nor less mysterious than that. His father, a lawyer, had his heart set on seeing his son follow in his career but, on the evening before the opening of school, Eugenio Pacelli announced his plans for entering the priesthood. Sometime, during his visits to St. Peter's and somewhere, during his walks and meditations among the shrines and tombs of Rome, he met the Christ.

Ordained at the age of twenty-three, he insisted he wanted nothing more than to emulate the Blessed Master. While his talents did not permit him to live the sheltered life, it was well known that during his career from priest to Pope his constant prayer was, "Keep me humble in spirit and steadfast in faith."

His path crossed the path of the Man from Nazareth and he made a disposition of Him. He made of Him a Divine Authority. He had that kind of mind.

Therese Neumann made of the Nazarene a Sentiment and an Emotion; Shoghi Effendi made of Him a Prophet; Pacelli made of Him a Divine Authority.

That is where he took his place in the circle of faith. The sovereignty of Jesus ruled his life. The dictates of Jesus became his prerogative. The supremacy of Jesus governed his actions.

Had Pacelli lived in Jesus' time, he would have followed Him then as unquestioningly as the Swiss guards follow and protect the Holy Father today. Jesus would have been for him what He was for Peter, "The Christ, the Son of the Living God." Like Paul, Pacelli would have made the lowly Galilean the monarch of this world and of the world to come. For him it would have been preposterous ever to have thought that Jesus did not actually have an earthly empire in mind or that He did not desire the pomp and pageantry which the Church now offers Him.

It is this seizure upon Divine Authority that justifies Pius XII in playing his impossible dual role of emperor and monk. It is because of this that he believes secular and spiritual power are conterminous in the holy life. There is no room for speculation in this type of mind, no place for varying shades of meaning. "Thus saith the Lord" is blazed above the apostolic path and must always be remembered as the unquestioned motto of the Vatican State during the reign of this scholarly king.

Many another Pope, under the merciless judgment of the non-Catholic world, has been dubbed with nicknames ranging from the "Red Dragon" to the "Whore of Babylon," but the worst that will ever be said of Pope Pius XII is that he was the crusader for Divine Authority. On this point, and this alone, he has sought to woo Protestantism. With diplomatic persuasion, he has taught the children of every faith that civil rights must conform to the laws of God, and that the primary principles of social relationships are to "live together in order and live together in tranquillity." There has never been a Pope who believed as sincerely as does Pius XII that Protestantism has already endorsed his views for peace and his plans for charity and justice.

The Divine Authority for which he speaks fuses all mankind into one holy pattern. Others may regard this as rank assumption and an unholy indignity, but he claims it is the fire at the heart of the altar of Christian faith. He speaks as though he were the watchman over the entire world. His topics are of gigantic scope. He addresses himself to industry on the technological concept of life;

to governments, on the hydrogen bomb; to the schismatic Eastern Church on the need for reunion; to physicists, on germ warfare; to parents, on birth control; to labor, on a living wage and the right to organize.

Again and again he has called a warring, suffering world to remember Divine Authority and has said, "When Jesus was crucified there was darkness over all the earth. This is a terrifying symbol of what still happens spiritually wherever incredulity, blind and proud of itself, has succeeded in excluding Christ from modern life, especially from public life, and has undermined Faith in God as well as Faith in Christ."

But never did he speak more eloquently or reveal himself more fully than when he addressed himself to the workers and laborers of Christendom. Never did he more clearly reflect his view of Jesus than when he said, "Our Saviour, Worker like you in His earthly life, was obedient to the Father even unto death. . . . In your workshops and factories, under the sun in the fields, in the darkness of the mines, amid the heat of the furnaces, wherever the word of Him Who Commands may call, may there descend upon you the abundance of His favors which may afford you help, safety, and solace, and make meritorious of another-world happiness the hard work in which you spend and sacrifice your life. Never doubt it! Christ is always with you. He is passing among you, noting your toil, listening to your conversations, consoling your hearts, composing your disagreements. You shall see the workshop changed into the sanctuary of Nazareth; and there will reign among you that trust, order and concord, which are a reflection of the blessing of Heaven that increases here below and conserves justice and good will among men who are steadfast in faith, in hope, and in the love of God."

His path crossed the path of the Man from Nazareth and he made of Him a Divine Authority. He has that type of mind.

6.

ALBERT SCHWEITZER

1.

Finally there was Albert Schweitzer.

Long before I met him I knew that he was a great man, with a greatness that touched people in all walks of life. One summer afternoon a road worker who came down to my British Columbia cabin for a drink of water spied a book on my table. It was Schweitzer's *Out of My Life and Thought.*

"That's good reading," he commented.

"You've heard of him?" I asked, for this was long before Schweitzer became internationally known and ten years before he received the 1952 Nobel Peace Award.

With a show of pride the laborer said, "Come up to my home some time and see my Schweitzer library."

I went up. Back in the hills of the Kootenay country, road foreman Lawson Hepher had books by and about Schweitzer that I had never seen. More than that, the writings had given quiet and meaning to his life. Years ago, a Mrs. Lillian Russell, who had worked with Schweitzer and translated much of his material, had visited in the British Columbia region. Through her the people of the valley and the hills were introduced to the Schweitzer personality. They never met *him,* but they met one who reflected him and who imparted to them something of his spirit.

It always seemed to me that no one came nearer to a definition of Schweitzer's influence in the world than did Mr. Hepher. He said, "Schweitzer is great because he has the courage to do what we would do if we had the courage."

I thought of this whenever an accolade for Schweitzer was noted in the press and whenever he was acclaimed in pulpit or lecture hall. Several times on TV shows when people were asked whom they would like most to be, they said, "That man in Africa, Albert Schweitzer."

Ministers spoke of him as the Protestant saint. Editorials referred to him as "our greatest living contemporary." Articles about him were titled, "The Man with the Cosmic Mind," "Man of Mercy," "The Man of the Century." French movies told his story and the radio brought his experiences into the comfort of American homes. Like everyone else, I had a secret feeling that by applauding him I was fulfilling a certain mission for my time; by living vicariously in the rugged and selfless ministry of this luminous figure, I was paying a debt of service to my fellowman. It all came back to this: "Schweitzer is great because he has the courage to do what we would do if we had the courage."

I suppose it was this unpaid debt to an inner compulsion that made me set off to French Equatorial Africa where, in the midst of disease and need, the Schweitzer we have glorified has worked for more than forty devoted years. I went as the average American would go, the easy way; by jet plane from Cairo to Johannesburg, by DC-6 from Johannesburg to Libreville, by DC-2 from

Libreville to a makeshift landing strip on the equatorial airfield called Lambaréné.

Here where the natives still gather around to see the plane which flies in three times a week, where refueling is done by hand, and where few passengers come unless they have Schweitzer in mind, a truck was waiting to take us (Mrs. Bach and myself) some five miles to the bank of the Ogooué River. It was comfort, or nearly so, all the way. The dirt road was serviceable and the February weather, though generating a treacherous heat, was no worse than an oppressive summer's day in the American Midwest.

We were met at the Ogooué by one of Schweitzer's most devoted helpers, Miss Emma Haussknecht, who was in her thirtieth year of service as nurse in the Schweitzer hospital and secretary on the Schweitzer staff. Her strength and competence left no doubt about the kind of qualities the jungle doctor inspired in those who worked with him. Dressed in white, wearing a white pith helmet over her gray hair, she was fit and sturdy, and obviously no ordinary individual. Neither was this an ordinary land. Where the single country road ended, an improvised ferry was waiting to carry the truck across the half-mile stretch of muddy water to the little closed-in settlement of Lambaréné.

Here, where we stood, the dense and tangled wilderness had been halted abruptly by the flooded stream and as I viewed the scene a vision of this country as seen from the air leaped into mind. Lorena, my wife, had photographed it from the plane all the way from Libreville.

The pictures would show an intricate web of water and vegetation, a labyrinth of everglades untamed and unexplored. Since coming to Africa a month previously, we had flown over countless miles of this feverish, forgotten waste, and here at the river's edge the rusty current was like the crooked spine of a jungle giant, bared defiantly to the beating sun. Here ran the quivering nerves of the dark land. Here where Schweitzer came forty years ago because its "people needed help the most," here where he brought his touch of healing and faith, the region itself seemed to bear the marks of pain.

Miss Haussknecht had brought two umbrellas and warned us that the sun was deceptive. With confidence and authority, she instructed the three native boys to push the dugout canoe slightly from the sandy shore, then steady it until we were seated, umbrellas up, our light pieces of baggage stowed around our knees. She gave her orders in a native dialect and the boys, gripping long paddles in their glossy black hands, shoved off. To the accompaniment of shrill, barbaric shouts they set up a rowing rhythm that sent the paddles digging lustily into the yellow stream.

This was the country which Schweitzer had described as "antediluvian scenery." What we were seeing was a preview of what the Ogooué was like throughout its headlong course of nearly a thousand miles. This was a smitten land where God had used the leftovers from his work of creation. Grotesque growths of palms and papyrus clumps, twisted and knotted together with the exotic bush-ropes, were squeezed into the rusty, cloggy water.

Strangling arms of gray-green clutched at every still-breathing bush and bracken, to form a macabre paradise for whatever soul-less denizens could here survive. No doubt, the same hippopotami, crocodiles, reptiles, and crustaceans that had greeted Schweitzer nearly a half century ago were still here, and the chatter and songs of the monkeys and birds seemed merely the echoes of what he had then heard in these dense green crypts.

But the forward surge of the narrow, homemade skiff and the presence of Miss Haussknecht sitting regally before us presented another impression equally strong. A conquering spirit had come into this land. A presence, vividly felt, was here and, given time, it would take this raw, unfinished stuff of creation and show the world the glory of perfect, finished things. The boatmen's sharp, high-pitched cries were like an overture to that day. Dugout canoes that sped downstream in the native traffic of the Ogooué hinted that here was a certain beauty which only spirit vision could discern. "We are living as God made us in the land where God placed us," the natives seemed to say, and in their life and death existence they expressed an enviable attitude of fatalistic freedom.

"There," said Miss Haussknecht, "is a sight even I have rarely seen."

She was calling our attention to a houseboat, an unsteady but spacious raft, covered with earth and vegetation and bearing somewhat off-center a crudely built thatched hut. This amazing spectacle floated peaceably down the river like a slice of meadowland loosed by a flood. Seated around the hut was a native family, the mother calmly nursing a child at her breast.

Lorena's camera clicked and as the crusted plot of earth drifted by, my thoughts went back to another greensward which I had visited recently, a greensward where other children had played long ago. My thoughts were back in Günsbach in Alsace where Schweitzer had spent his boyhood. He was born in Upper Alsace at Kaysersberg on January 14, 1875, but it was Günsbach, where his father was the Evangelical pastor, that he called home. I had gone there, moved by sentiment, to get the feeling of the quiet village streets, to visit the church where, at the age of nine, young Albert played the organ, and to walk where he had spent his happy youth with three sisters and a younger brother.

What a contrast that hushed and peaceful town, with its reverent hills and sturdy homes, was to this tangled land! Could it really be that Schweitzer had come here because the days of his boyhood had been so blessed? Was this a debt he was paying to humanity and to God for all he had enjoyed and received during the first thirty-odd years of his life? Had he come here because of a spiritual pain that had tormented him as a youth?—the thought that while he had so much in health, talent, and ease there were those who knew only disease and want? Was this the answer to the Schweitzer riddle? A remembrance of the steepled church and the stately manse at Günsbach blurred my vision as I watched the houseboat drift away into watery jungle space.

Miss Haussknecht was speaking to the boys at the oars.

"Shout a bit louder," she told them, "so that the good doctor will hear you."

Their cries rose to resounding shrieks. They were laughing inwardly as they speared their paddles into the stream and sent the boat toward a clearing far upward on the Lambaréné side. We could make out several long, low buildings. We could see a compound, and laundry drying where it had been draped over bushes and shrubs. Several natives were moving about in the dense foliage of the shore, but presently we caught sight of a white-clad figure moving with strong and steady steps down the swathed-out path that led to the improvised muddy dock. A white jungle helmet was pushed back on his head. As he stood watching while we approached it seemed to me that he might have been standing there for forty years, his back to the wilderness and his searching eyes gazing out across the world.

I glanced at Lorena and knew what she was thinking: "Oh, for a picture!"

I shook my head. But a mental photograph was registered as Schweitzer lifted his hand in greeting and came closer to the bank as our boat squashed into the soggy, yellow beach. He extended his hand and assisted us as we stepped out into this humid "paradise" of mahogany and oil-palm trees.

"Welcome!" he exclaimed in German. "This is different transportation than you are accustomed to."

The touch of humor and the twinkle in his eyes put us at ease. My German, for which I apologized, satisfied him. He was glad we had made the trip and I felt that this first moment had already rewarded me, and had partially answered some of the obvious questions: why is he here, what kind of man is he, what does he believe and why does he believe it?

There are those whose very presence is a testimonial of inner conviction and Schweitzer is one of these. You feel his great humanitarianism; you sense his moral responsibility; and you know with certainty that he is captive to his calling. It seemed to me that the Schweitzer riddle was already half solved the moment I put my hand in his.

2.

First of all, here was a person who, despite his extravagant "advance notices" and his near deification by the press and public, came up to all expectations. Here was a man who carried greatness with humility, and strength with gentleness. Those who had described him as being of indeterminate age were right. He might have been fifty-five instead of past eighty and only his drooping gray mustache gave a hint of the generation to which he belonged. My German father had a mustache like that, a kind of Bismarckian trait that left no question about whose word was law, but which also suggested a subtle winsomeness that drew us into his arms.

Schweitzer gave us an immediate impression of fatherliness; and his easy, natural manner, coupling grace with self-discipline, and dignity with vigor, made anyone wish to be drawn into his circle of affection. He was a man of more than average height and strong physique; but it was his nature that impressed us, his sensitivity and frankness, and his spontaneous acceptance of us. It was almost as if by our coming we, too, had a share in his mission and work.

Yes, the answer to the question, "What makes this man great," began to unfold even as we started up the narrow path to begin our Lambaréné stay. "He has the courage to do what we would do if we had the courage," was only a small part of it. Schweitzer is great for three reasons, and the first of these is the obvious one: *he has taken the talents which life has given him and sublimated them in the talent of human service.*

You realize this the moment you meet him. Here is the man who has been acknowledged as the world's greatest authority on Johann Sebastian Bach. He has written about him with such insight, sensitivity, and understanding that some say Schweitzer must be an incarnation of this master of the choral prelude and fugue, this man whom he refers to as "not a single but a universal personality."

He is Bach's translator, his spiritual amanuensis, the abbot over the Bach basilica. Critics will tell you that when Schweitzer plays Bach it is as though Bach himself were playing it. But it is not this that makes him great. You know it is not when he pauses for a moment at the door of the hospital which he built, most of it with his own hands, and quietly warns, "I would not touch anything, for we have diseases here which are hardly known in your country."

You enter close behind him. You find yourself in a hospital where the beds are plain straw matting. The walls are sheet iron. Instead of running water there are calabashes which hold the priceless liquid. You meet those who bear the signs of pain: the victims of elephantiasis, tumors, sleeping sickness, strangulated hernia and the ever present malaria, to say nothing of the mental diseases.

You see something besides the evidences of suffering. You see an inner light reaching out from the eyes of the sick as they gaze upward to the white-helmeted man. Understandingly he takes hold of a hand. He lays his palm on a fevered brow. He speaks words of encouragement as he moves among the two hundred patients crowded into this infirmary, this city of refuge for those whom the world neglected or forgot.

Then you say to yourself, here is the man who is a genius not only in the field of music, but also in the field of scholarship. Here is one of the world's most respected authorities on Goethe. As long ago as 1928 he received from the city of Frankfort the Goethe prize, the highest possible recognition of its kind. His one visit to the United States was for the purpose of delivering a Goethe oration at Aspen, Colorado, in 1949. The money he received for this went into his hospital work at Lambaréné.

You remember this as he takes you into the small surgical and pharmaceutical rooms where a trusted native worker is tidying things up and where there is good evidence that much more is needed in the way of equipment and supplies. Only Schweitzer's Alsatian thrift and his indomitable faith ever got this work started in the first place. Then, as now, he saved and put to use every piece of string, every carton, every crate, every precious piece of metal.

Famous as a musician, famous as a scholar, he is equally famous as a physician and surgeon. And the moment you say this, you remember that he has a fourth universal talent, for he is acclaimed by those who agree with him, and by those who do not, as one who stands pre-eminent among the philosophers and theologians of his time. Who among the clergy has not read his *Civilization and Ethics, The Quest of the Historical Jesus, Paul and His Interpreters, The Mystery of the Kingdom of God?* In how many universities and seminaries are his conclusions being discussed at this very moment? Long ago he started a battle in the field of religion and ethics and trained no other general than himself to lead the fight.

He did train himself. He took his philosophical conclusions and his theological beliefs, he took his musical art, his scholarship, and his surgical skill—he took his four talents and went, quietly and without fanfare, out of the luxury of Europe into the poverty of the Dark Continent. He went, not out of the world, but into it. It was not a flight from suffering, but an assault upon suffering; not an escape, but a mission; and he went not as one superior to those whom he sought to help, but as a comrade in the quest for ways to heal their suffering and their pain.

Early in his narrative, *Out of My Life and Thought,*

he wrote, "I wanted to be a doctor that I might be able to work without having to talk. For years I have been giving myself out in words, and it was with joy that I had followed the calling of theological teacher and preacher. But this new form of activity I could not represent to myself as *talking* about the religion of love, but only as an actual putting of it into practice."

As I recalled these words in Lambaréné and as I got to know Schweitzer the man, the thought came to me, "If all the sermonizers and all the radio preachers and all the would-be reformers and platform lecturers would stop their preaching and start living the life they preach, without thought of glory or gain, what a sudden impact would be made upon society and our time!" And as I reflected on this, the contagion of the Schweitzer spirit rushed over me once more. What was *I* ready to do? What talents did *I* have that could be gathered together and put to work in human service? For I, too, had made ideas a substitute for deeds and had preferred pronouncements to personal action. Now I was confronted by one whose ideas had impelled him to invest his life in a cause, whose pronouncements had as their aim service instead of advice. It was not the lack of vision, but the lack of courage and will that had held me back.

Lambaréné needed doctors. It did not need visitors or guests. The "average man" could only be in the way, and I was an average man. But as we met the members of the Schweitzer staff, four doctors and ten nurses and helpers, all of whom donate their time in complete disregard for self or praise, it became clearer to me what this sublimation of talent meant. It meant that where the sum total of a man's abilities meet the world's need, that was where God had called him. It might mean a jungle in French Equatorial Africa, but it also meant one's home town. It meant not only a Schweitzer, it meant an "average man"—any and every man who dared to have the courage to take his talents and put them to work in fulfilling the needs of men.

During my stay in Lambaréné I felt that the Schweitzer story should be left to his biographers, but the Schweitzer message and its inspiration should be identified with and demonstrated by everyone who pretends to minister in the name of Christ. For Lambaréné is a laboratory and a proving ground for the great command, "Preach the Word, heal the sick, cast out devils!" And what had been discovered here would have to be repeated in the jungles of civilization before that great new day of a great new world would ever dawn.

Schweitzer put it this way, "The only way out of today's misery is for people to be worthy of each other's trust."

It is doubtful whether he could have achieved what he did in this primeval land unless he had been willing to pool all of his talents. Only as a musician could he have detected the symphony of this region where stinging heat and tornadoes are flung from Nature's hand in a kind of *Götterdämmerung.*

Only as a poet could he sense the varying cadences of this life with its listless pace suddenly shocked into terror by some unanticipated happening. The swirl of the

Ogooué would surely need to creep like poetry into one's soul before the jaundiced river could be looked upon as a friend.

Only as a philosopher and a mystic would a man be able to adjust himself to a universe that is and shall ever remain mysterious and transcendent and then believe with all his heart that the mysterious and transcendent in man is an expression of the Real. He must love life with all its torturous afflictions and love God without being able to comprehend the total meaning of suffering and pain.

Only as a doctor of medicine who is at heart also a physician of souls could Schweitzer ask for no other joy and reward than to see the lepers cleansed, suffering bodies eased, and demons cast out of bedeviled minds. It must ever be said of this man that he took his four supreme talents and sublimated them in the one surpassing talent of human service. This was the first ingredient I discovered in his universal greatness.

3.

There was a second reason for Schweitzer's greatness: *He has a philosophy of life and it is not one of words alone, but of action.* By this time, his "reverence for life" is better known than Plato's "form of the Good," than Kant's "laws of thought," or Hegel's "unity of self with the not-self." The reason Schweitzer's philosophy is better known is because he has demonstrated it.

His is not a philosophy of the lips but of life. Where others have pieced together and integrated knowledge, he has made philosophy a living force by example. This is his imitation of Christ, and to the Christ consciousness he gives full credit for his inspiration.

This personal influence, real and definable, was something I immediately felt and it made me impatient to return to my world and there test my courage in my field of work against the courage of this man. His unforgettable words, spoken almost as an aside, "Example is the only way to influence others," were an illumination for my path as nothing had ever been before, simply because Schweitzer actualized them. Here at Lambaréné natives were bringing the sick on crude litters through jungle paths, and the maimed and the suffering on boats and rafts because *Oganda*—the Christian medicine man—had said, "Come, we are ready to help you."

When I saw all this I was tormented by the fact that all through my life, my philosophy, such as it was, had been mostly academic, a point of view to be talked about, and defended, and discussed—rarely lived, hardly ever lived as a selfless, determining force. Here was Schweitzer, defending what he believed by working as if the belief were true, demonstrating it in acts of charity.

Here, he directed the work of building a new shed, sleeves rolled up, hat pushed back on his head, showing the native workmen how a job should be done.

There, he was pulling up weeds or sinking a spade into the trampled ground, planting, planning, not for himself but for those who might one day perpetuate his ideal of service. I saw him in the hospital wards and with the members of the patients' families who usually come along with the sick one and squat around the hospital doors. They prepare their meals over little charcoal fires and help with the laundering. They could be, and perhaps often are, very much in the way. Schweitzer is strong-willed as he deals with them and instructs them, but he never fails to reveal his basic reverence for life.

He stated his proposition in his *Ethics*. "It is in reverence for life that knowledge passes over into experience. . . . Life bears its meaning in itself. And this meaning is to be found in living out the highest and most worthy idea which my will-to-live can furnish . . . the idea of reverence for life." Lambaréné helped me to understand the full impact of these words, though I had read them many times and found them easily quotable.

The natives trust Schweitzer as no white man in Africa has ever been trusted. They love him, but what is more important is their conviction that he loves them. He loves them even when they abuse him, when they forget to thank him, when they insult him, when they steal from him.

Often in the jungle one who had been healed returned to his village of grass huts and told his story. "There is that man, the *Oganda,* the *Grand Docteur,* who came long years ago and was from the beginning different from other men. He asks nothing for himself. He does not command us to change our way of life. He does not mock us for what we believe. He comes as if once, before the memory of men, he might himself have been one of our own people. There was only one small hut at Lambaréné when he and his wife came up the Ogooué that first time. But there was also a chicken house. This he made into his hospital and it was here that we learned what kind of a man he was. Here our people who were very sick came to him. *Oganda* often put them to sleep and when they woke up the pain was gone and they were sick no longer. Some day you will meet the *Grand Docteur* and you will know when you see him that he is a good man. How will you know? You will feel his goodness and you will see it in all that he does."

Such native response was but an echo of my own. It was also the honest, simple reaction of the members of the staff who, like Emma Haussknecht, have never lost their awe and respect for their chief. I felt this as I ate at the long friendly family table where Schweitzer sits at the center surrounded by those who have entered the fellowship of his service. I was made aware of it when I went with any one of the group on a round of duty. I sensed it when a Bach chorale mingled with the night sounds of the jungle land.

There is no organ at Lambaréné, but in a small, homey room Schweitzer has his cherished upright piano with organ foot pedals attached. This instrument, a gift from the Paris Bach Society, much worn and much used, is Schweitzer's most prized possession. At this antique instrument he takes his place, he who could be sitting at the greatest cathedral in Europe. Americans, who are constantly urging him to tour the States, have long been asking, "What's he doing at Lambaréné? How long does he expect to stay? Who's there that understands or appreciates him?"

In the mellow light of candles burning in the sconces on the piano panel, you find the answer. He is doing at Lambaréné what God called him to do. He will stay as long as he can, as long as he has the strength.

For whom does he play? For any of the natives who may listen out of curiosity or desire. He played for Lorena and me, for the members of his staff; and there was no doubt in my mind that he was also playing for every form of life from his aged cat to his proud pet pelican. Perhaps, most of all, he plays for the God he serves. His recognition of and reflection upon the fact that everything in the universe has a "will to live" could bring him to no other conclusion than that the entire spectrum of life is sacred and worthy of his art.

That is why I say he is great. He lives out his philosophy of life. Like Goethe, he insists that thought and conduct must be one.

He tells how, long ago, as a boy in Günsbach, he went with a companion during the closing days of Lent to engage in the common sport of shooting birds. Armed with slingshots, they crept close to a tree in which the birds were singing. His young friend raised his weapon and instructed Albert to do the same. Schweitzer says he loaded the slingshot and took aim. Just then the bells of the church began to ring. The sound was like a "voice from heaven" and obeying it, he sprang to his feet and shooed the birds away. With his customary candor, and unashamed of his emotion, he reported that the music of the bells that day "drove deep into my heart the commandment, 'Thou shalt not kill.' "

In this same account of his childhood he relates how, after his mother had prayed the evening prayer and kissed him good night, he would silently add a prayer of his own, "Oh, heavenly Father, protect and bless all things that have breath; guard them from all evil, and let them sleep in peace."

He grew to love all living things and there was planted in his heart the belief that it was wrong to inflict suffering and death if they could by any means be avoided. His faithfulness to this inner light often made him the object of reproach and ridicule.

Stories began to circulate that he let rats and mice out of traps. "If there are ants on his table," someone reported, "Albert will brush them gently to the floor and then feed them crumbs." In the French movie, *Il Est Minuit*, this attitude was stressed by showing his reluctance to kill the insects and creeping things when first he came to Lambaréné. Lorena and I had seen this film at a theater in Colmar, a city ten miles from Günsbach. Occasionally, throughout the showing, a man beside me leaned over and commented, "Yes, that is our Albert Schweitzer. That is just what he would do. Yes, he is that way when it comes to animals. He loves all living things."

I thought of *Il Est Minuit* as I watched Schweitzer affectionately caring for his aged cat which had already lost its teeth. He fed it mush. The old cat still had a "will to live." Lorena took a picture of him with his pet pelican and his antelope, and one of two baby gorillas which a staff doctor had acquired as special pets. The longer I was with Schweitzer the more I believed in St. Francis of Assisi. And it may be that until the masses of men retain such childlike trust and affection for life on every scale, we never will see the kingdom of God on earth.

4.

The boyhood episode of the birds and the Angelus bells was to find a recurrent note when Schweitzer, as a student, became interested in Hindu philosophy. What his heart had found despite the world of European materialism, he now rediscovered as pure revelation in the Upanishads and the Gita. What had been revealed to him as an insight into a modern spiritual culture was now spread out before him in ancient Indian thought. In Hinduism's Vedanta he recognized the essence of life not as fixed forms or creedal patterns, not even as philosophical reflections, but as religious practice.

Among Hinduism's Jains he found the doctrine of *Ahimsa* which forbids the taking of life in any form. It was the Jains' prophet Mahavira who had said, "Do not kill any living thing, or hurt any living thing by word, thought or deed. Do not kill animals. Do not kill the lowliest creature. Do not step upon a worm. Do not kill the mosquito that bites you or the bee that stings you. Do not go to war. Do not fight your attacker. Follow *Ahimsa!* Do no injury to anything that possesses a soul."

Far from ridiculing the Jains and their doctrine, Schweitzer went beyond the surface exhibition of their concepts and practices and found, with characteristic insight, the spiritual justification for their beliefs. He saw no conflict between Christianity and Jainism so far as the ethical basis of *Ahimsa* was concerned.

Bluntly and with customary disregard for his critics, Schweitzer said, "The laying down of the commandment not to kill and not to harm is one of the greatest events in the spiritual history of mankind. Starting from its principle, founded on world and life denial, of abstention from action, Indian thought reaches the tremendous discovery that ethics know no bounds. So far as we know, this is for the first time clearly expressed by Jainism."

He was on his way up the Ogooué in September, 1915, when the revelation came to him that broke through the "iron door" which had stood so long between the understanding of a philosophy of civilization and an attitude toward the world. He was the only passenger on a small steamer that was towing a barge and the object of the one hundred sixty mile upstream trip was to reach the ailing wife of a missionary. He relates how he sat on the deck, among a crew of natives, how they shared their food with him, and how he spent most of the time wrestling with his search for the "elementary and universal conception of the ethical." This was the iron door. It had refused to yield to any clear-cut phraseology. What was the conceivable but inaccessible goal that it hid from him? Was a man to accept the fact that the will to believe and the will to do were merely attitudes and illusions handed down through time? Or did these actually arise anew in each generation and in each individual as a spiritual reality?

For three days he struggled with the problem and then, in words typical of his narrative style, he says, "At the very moment when, at sunset, we were making our way through a herd of hippopotamuses, there flashed upon my mind, unforeseen and unsought, the phrase, 'Reverence for Life.' The iron door had yielded; the path in the thicket had become visible. Now I had found my way to the idea in which world- and life-affirmation and ethics are contained side by side! Now I knew that the world view of ethical world- and life-affirmation, together with the ideals of civilization, is founded in thought."

Simply stated, the concept of a "Reverence for Life" was from the start based upon the reflection that the will to live is instinctive in human beings, but not in human beings alone, but in every living thing. To thinking man this instinct becomes the spiritual cohesive of all of life. It joins men in a common thought and enjoins upon them a common ethic, a respect for each man's will to live. Man's daily affirmation should be, "I am life which wills to live, in the midst of life which wills to live."

Schweitzer's ethical acceptance of the world and life

will continue to be debated long and loud in the ivied halls of learning around the world. Literary critics and essayists will have their say about the distinctive character of his thought and by academic juggling will pigeonhole him along with other philosophers old and new. A battle is already raging around his "heresies" and there are those who will make a name and a career for themselves simply by talking about his beliefs, analyzing his mind, and deifying or dissecting his personality. But his greatest interpreter will be the man of action whose call will take him into the world of need and there, by means of love and knowledge, minister with a Schweitzer-like reverence for life in the spirit of the Christ.

5.

All of which brought me to another discovery of Schweitzer's greatness, for there is something else that makes the man of Lambaréné our most influential contemporary. This third ingredient can be put into a simple, understandable phrase: Schweitzer is great because, *throughout his life, he continually gave a little more and did a little more than the world expected of him.*

When Lorena and I walked with him to the leper colony a short distance from the main hospital, we came suddenly upon an orange grove planted in the midst of the jungle. Pausing as we neared it, Schweitzer said, "A man begins to feel old when he sees the trees that he has planted bearing fruit."

I ventured to say, "Yes, but you will have a good crop." The oranges were hanging thick and green on the trees.

"I will be fortunate if I get a dozen of those oranges," he replied.

"Why? What will happen to them?"

"They will be stolen."

"Who would steal them?" I asked.

"The natives."

"Those whom you have helped and healed? What makes them do it?"

"That's a good question," he reflected. "I asked one of the men once, 'Why do you steal my oranges?' He said, 'If I don't steal them, someone else will!' "

There was grave humor in this remark, but I thought of it as quite symbolic of the Schweitzer life. He will go on —even though they steal his oranges. He will continue to give a little more than the world expects or his work demands of him. The story of his life will ever be the story of this *plus* factor and while we find it demonstrated most graphically at Lambaréné, it has been and is still present in every chapter of his experiences.

It figured in his determination to come to the mission station in the first place. At that time (1913) the Paris Missionary Society had serious misgivings about his theology. He was an unorthodox liberal and what would he do about the saving of souls? Little did the Society suspect how much *more* this man would do than merely preach a way of salvation. He would demonstrate it. He would show that a man is "saved" when he gives not only his soul but his body to the call of Christ. His sermons were not preached, they were demonstrated. Goethe said it and Schweitzer proved it: "In the beginning was the Deed!" Jesus commanded it and Schweitzer obeyed it: "Heal the sick and say unto them, 'The Kingdom of God is come nigh unto you!' "

Yes, Schweitzer is great because he does more than is expected of him. And he *believes* more fervently than others do because the roots of his faith are thrust deep into religious truth wherever truth is found. He is not a sentimentalist, though his heart is easily and quickly moved by acts of kindness on the part of others. The one who returns to thank him wins a special place in his affection, but he confidently understands those who do not return, for he has already explained that the "thankless lepers" whom Jesus healed were actually not thankless. They may simply have had so many other duties to perform that they could not return and show their appreciation.

Tears came to his eyes when, in my presence, he received a small and unexpected gift for his hospital work. "To think this should be done for me," was his whispered comment.

He is not an idealist, though his dreams form a very real part of his everyday life. As for his service to the natives, this he has always looked upon not merely as a "good work" but as the partial payment of a debt which the white man owes to the oppressed and exploited black. Despite disappointments received at their hands, despite their untrustworthiness, their lassitude, their cruelty to animals and their superstitions, Schweitzer emphatically declares, "There lives within him (the native) a dim suspicion that a correct view of what is truly good must be attainable as the result of reflection. In proportion as he becomes familiar with the higher moral ideas of the religion of Jesus, he finds utterance for something within himself that has hitherto been dumb, and something that has been tightly bound up finds release. The longer I live among the Ogooué Negroes, the clearer this becomes to me."

It was the white man and not the black who brought the first break in Schweitzer's vocation. World War I reached into the jungle in August, 1914, by means of the long arm of the French military and interned the Alsatian doctor and his wife as aliens on the mission grounds. Schweitzer was ordered to have no association with the natives and no hospital activities. But they could not keep him from creative work. It was during this period that he began his monumental three-volume *Philosophy of Civilization.* Neither could his "imprisonment" break the spiritual bond between him and the jungle people; soon he was the trusted friend of the native guards. Nor could his captors keep the sick from pounding at his door, and in due time he was allowed to practice almost as freely as before.

In 1917, he and his wife were shipped off to Europe as civilian internes and placed in prisoner-of-war camps, first at Garaison in the Pyrenees and months later at St.

Remy de Provence. What did these experiences do to his reverence for life? How did he now react to the "plus factor" in the field of human service?

At no time does the spirit of the man reveal itself more clearly than in the long months when commands and trumpet signals herded them back and forth across the prison grounds, and when men broke under the agony of "walking round and round looking out over the walls at the glorious, white shimmering chain of the Pyrenees." But he discovered that he was the only physician among these men and soon the authorities gave him permission to do what he could to stamp out the sickness and misery inside the confining walls. Mrs. Schweitzer, who had not been well and had already suffered much physical discomfort in Lambaréné, grew worse during the unbearable oppression at St. Remy. Schweitzer himself became the victim of severe attacks of fever. In 1918, worn and broken, they were informed that an exchange of prisoners would eventually bring them back to their beloved Alsace, to Günsbach in the Münster valley.

Schweitzer tells a story about this release which was later—more than thirty years later—to bear upon an incident in America during his Aspen visit. He relates how he and his wife dragged themselves wearily from the St. Remy camp to the station at Tarascon, where weak and loaded with baggage, they could hardly make their way to the train. "Thereupon a poor cripple," Schweitzer says, "whom I had treated in the camp came forward to help us. He had no baggage because he possessed nothing, and I was much moved by his offer, which I accepted. While we walked along side by side in the scorching sun, I vowed to myself that in memory of him I would in the future always keep a lookout at stations for heavily laden people, and help them. This vow I have kept."

He kept it so well that, during his Chicago stop on his way to Colorado, while standing with a group of professors and admirers awaiting his train, he spied a woman lugging her heavy bags. "Excuse me, gentlemen," he said, and off he went to help her with her suitcases. The cripple at Tarascon was not forgotten. His determination that example is the only way to influence others took precedence over erudite talk about philosophy and faith.

Schweitzer does not easily forget. Back in Alsace, in the aftermath of the war, he could not give up his dreams and his thoughts about Lambaréné. A serious operation which he had to undergo in a Strasbourg hospital, a need for money, and even the realization that Mrs. Schweitzer might never again be able to endure the African climate —all these could not blot from his mind the natives and their needs. "How fond one becomes of them, in spite of all the trouble they give!" he once exclaimed. "How many beautiful traits of character we can discover in them, if we refuse to let the many and varied follies of the child of nature prevent us from looking for the man in him! How they disclose to us their real selves, if we have love and patience enough to understand them!"

Still working toward turning the dream into reality, Schweitzer lectured in Europe and England on philosophy and religion, but the words he spoke went back to an experience on an Ogooué river barge. He wrote on the mysticism of Paul and on world religions, but first he wrote *On the Edge of the Primeval Forest,* the story of the jet-black children to whom God had given a torturous but beautiful land.

He gave organ recitals in churches and in concert halls, but haunting him were the chants of the natives as he had heard them in the days when he labored where few white men had ever been. The support of the Mission Society had been withdrawn. The war had changed things. The world had taken on new attitudes. He was told there was enough work of reconstruction and rehabilitation to be done in Europe. Günsbach itself had been torn by the crossfire of artillery; but always there was Lambaréné where, in the toil and travail of his first divine appointment, Schweitzer had found the pearl of great price—a reverence for life.

In 1924, aided by friends' gifts which supplemented fees received from lectures and recitals, he was able to pay the debts he owed the Paris Missionary Society, and once more embarked from Bordeaux for the month long journey to Port Gentil at the mouth of the Ogooué. Mrs. Schweitzer had to remain in Europe for reasons of health and with her stayed their only child, a daughter, Rhena.

It was the Easter season in 1924 when the *Grand Docteur* returned. The conquering jungle, which knew no reverence for any life excepting its own, had strangled the buildings and over-run the sites. Schweitzer again became a builder and, through toil and faith and infinite patience with native help, slowly erected the present facilities where from his tiny, closet-like office, he looks out across the hospital grounds to see a modern answer to an ancient call that said, "Come unto me."

There are gardens growing in the great forest now which supply vegetables and even some coffee and grain. Goats which provide an ample supply of milk have the run of the "meadow" and chickens roam the compound. All of which, together with plantains and mangoes and other fruit offer food for the patients and the hospital staff. Since the patients cannot pay for their treatment and care, they give, as they are able, work and service in construction and upkeep of the hospital and grounds.

This attitude that I have called "giving a little more than the world or life expects of a man," was vividly demonstrated when Schweitzer took me to one of the three leper villages a half-mile from the main hospital grounds. Here about a hundred of the more than three hundred people, victims of this "cancer of the jungle," live in small bamboo and palm leaf huts.

Here I saw a scene that I would not soon forget. I saw the only American doctor on the Schweitzer staff treating the wounds of a number of lepers who lay before him in the relatively cool shade of a small thatched pavilion. Dr. Harvey Wyckoff was unforgettable because of his apparent youth, his ascetic appearance, his sensitive face, his gentle eyes. Dressed in white and wearing a white pith helmet, he looked so startlingly young that

I involuntarily asked, "What are you doing down here anyway? How is it that you are here?"

His reply, made gracious by a quiet, knowing smile, was brief, "I heard of Dr. Schweitzer."

What he was saying was this, "If this man of Alsace can do so much with his life, isn't there a little more that I can do with mine?"

6.

And that was the question I seriously put to myself during my Lambaréné stay. There is something about the Schweitzer greatness that rubs off on every man who comes into his presence—either through his personality, or his writings, or his music, or any other one of his other achievements.

Somehow, in the light of the physician of Lambaréné, many of the things which seem so devastatingly import-tant in the realm of dogma, lose their significance. Political machinations and jostlings for power, the everlasting consciousness that urges one to save face or to win a point in public esteem are suddenly unimportant. A new perspective, a new sense of values takes hold of one and makes one feel for a little while, at least, as Schweitzer does, "that everyone shall exert himself in that state of life in which he is placed, to practice true humanity towards his fellowmen. On that depends the future of mankind. Enormous values come to nothing every moment through the missing of opportunities, but the values which do get turned into will and deed mean wealth which must not be undervalued. . . . To unbind what is bound, to bring the underground waters to the surface; mankind is waiting and longing for such as can do that."

Scholars will argue about him long and loud, but the man on the street has already solved the Schweitzer riddle. Schweitzer is what he is and where he is because his path crossed the path of the Man from Nazareth. He met Him during his boyhood days at Günsbach, and later when, as a student, he declared, "I resolved to devote my life till I was thirty to the office of preacher, to science, and to music. If by that time, I would take a path of immediate service as a man to my fellowmen. . . . A chain of circumstances pointed out to me the road which led to the sufferers from leprosy and sleeping sickness in Africa." He met the Man from Nazareth and he made of Him *a way of life.*

That is where he belongs in the Circle of Faith.

Three things have made Albert Schweitzer great. He has taken his talents and sublimated them in the talent of human service. He has proved his philosophy of life in action. He has given a little more than the world and life expected of him. But there is one crowning greatness which every thinking and circumspect modern man can understand. Schweitzer is great in that he cannot be claimed by any one race or sect. Like the Man he met, he belongs to humanity. He belongs wherever the *spirit* of that Man strives to reveal itself despite all the streams of blood and bitterness which separate men of differing faiths. He cannot honestly be identified in any single Protestant group or any specific area of Catholic thought. He is not a sectarian Christian. He is not only carrying out the teaching of Jesus; he is part of the teaching. His hospital, his influence, and his work are His.

Schweitzer met the man from Nazareth and he made of Him *a way of life*. He has that kind of mind.

7.

THE DISCOVERY

At last I found myself nearer an understanding of the "why" behind our varieties of religious experiences. It came down to this: many minds, many faiths. And I discovered that though this Man from Nazareth might appear to be dividing the people, the *experiencing* of Him was the one unifying force among those who followed the Christian way. It was part of God's conspiracy to make this unforgettable Figure to be all things to all men.

Therese Neumann, who made of Him a Sentiment and an Emotion, was a dramatic type, similar to many other individuals and groups. Her response to Him was, for example, very much like that of the late Aimee Semple MacPherson. It might have been Therese speaking when Aimee said, "On Good Friday I die with Him and on Easter morning I rise to greet Him in the garden."

The revivalists, from Billy Sunday to Billy Graham, were also of the Therese type of mind. Their message and the justification of their methods were based upon the sublimation of their love in Him. That was the appeal I found not only in evangelistic auditoriums, but also in monasteries and convents, Catholic and non-Catholic alike. When would people realize that those who responded to sentiment and emotion in life would always respond to the sentiment and emotion in Him? Across the Therese type of mind was the philosophy of the maid of Konnersreuth spelled out in bold and glaring type: the real heroes are those who acknowledge their complete subjection to the One they love.

Shoghi Effendi, who made of Him a Prophet, was symbolic of another group of believers. Meet Shoghi and you will better understand the Mormon people and Jehovah's Witnesses and the Adventists and all the many other groups who have made of this Man from Nazareth a Prophet. This type of mind sends its adherents on zealous missionary journeys, inspires them to testify in summer sun or winter sleet, and urges them to the belief that God has called them to be His special spokesmen in these "latter days." When would we learn that those who see the world as operating according to a Scriptural timetable must see in Jesus a prophetic figure for our time.

Come into the tradition of Helen Keller who found in Jesus a Mystical Presence and you are in the spiritual company of those who seek the Real. Through the intellect and the soul they perpetuate the eternal quest. They are captives of the inner vision, but free to see and help the world's longing and the world's need. "Three things of the literal sense perish," said Swedenborg, "when the spiritual sense evolves: time, space and person." Humanity for them is the universal family of God. This is the Meister Eckhart, the Rufus Jones, the Gerald Heard type of mind. It cannot be coerced or bound by a dogmatic dimension. It has worlds within worlds for its laboratory and truth for its goal. Patiently it defines man's age-old relationship to the Christ: we must emulate Him in our acts, reflect Him in our thoughts, and manifest Him in our lives.

Meet Pope Pius XII and you will see that there is a type of mind which wants and needs Divine Authority. It is the mind of a John Henry Newman and a Clare Booth Luce, a John Keble and a Fritz Kreisler, a Henry S. Manning and a son of John Foster Dulles. I found it in a friend of mine who, upon his conversion to Roman Catholicism, affirmed: "Here are the answers. At last I know what to believe." You will find this type of mind in other individuals and groups, the followers of the Eastern Christian faith, the Anglicans, and also those who make up the large and growing Christian Science group. "Wherever I go," a Christian Scientist told me, "our services are always uniform, and wherever I meet Scientists, they always think alike." It is the Divine Authority type of mind.

And then there is the "way of life" type of mind—the Schweitzer type. It is the mind of religion at work, actively, among men, and we find it in all denominations and in all communions. Meeting the Man from Nazareth inspires this type of mind to do something with its belief. Now a man is no longer religious just because he feels religious or because he is interested in religion or even because he can discuss religion. Life becomes a "call," a "vocation," a "partnership" with God. With it a man visualizes and works for new social relations and a new and higher standard of world culture. Whether it is relief from pain or release from selfishness, the "way of life" type of mind passes that way and leaves the imprint of its presence. The leper in the jungle, or peace in our time: it is all the same. Religion is a way of life, and Christianity, it believes, is that life in action.

Many minds, many faiths. When would we learn this truth and be willing to say there is no faith higher or lower than another—that they are only different in their interpretation of what religion is and does?

For since I had met them all, and appreciated them all, and believed them all, the five types of minds rewarded me with a great discovery: religion, like truth, is a circle. It has no beginning and no end. All denominational expressions and types of minds are arcs in that circle of truth. No one can claim the whole circle, but each can rightly claim his part of it. And this I also discovered: the more we live selfishly in our small arc, the less we see the whole circle. My five personalities were great because they have each traveled *around* the circle. For how could Therese love Him without also serving Him, and how could Schweitzer serve Him without Sentiment and Emotion? How could Helen Keller know His Mystical Presence without wanting to make Him her way of life? How could Shoghi Effendi make Him a Prophet without also seeing in Him a Divine Authority? How could Pius XII make Him a Divine Authority unless he also made Him a Prophet? And so on, in every conceivable combination, each believer reflected something of the other. Suddenly there were minds within minds, arcs within arcs, hearts within hearts, and souls within souls in the everlasting rhapsody of faith.

The Man from Nazareth *had* proved Himself to be all

things to all men. He was beyond localization in any one individual or any one group. I was back where I had started: "the disposition he has made of Jesus" *did* cut through denominational loyalties. When would the world learn this obvious truth? And how could it be stated so that men would listen and understand?

I found an answer, an answer which Schweitzer had already put into words, words so magnificent and compelling that they rested upon my seeking like a benediction. It was as if he had drawn together all my impressions about this Man from Nazareth and put them into a living thought for each and every type of mind.

"He comes to us," he said, "as One unknown, without a name, as of old, by the lakeside, He came to those who knew Him not. He speaks to us the same word: 'Follow me!' and sets us to tasks which He has to fulfill for our time. He commands. And to those who obey Him, whether they be wise or simple, He will reveal Himself in the toils, the conflicts, the sufferings which they shall pass through in His fellowship. And, as an ineffable mystery, they shall learn in their own experience who He is."

That was how it seemed to me.

THE AUTHOR AND HIS BOOK

MARCUS BACH *was born in Sauk City, Wisconsin, on December 15, 1906, and received his early education there. He held a Rockefeller fellowship in research and creative writing from 1934 to 1936. He received his M.A. in 1937 and his Ph.D. in 1942 at the University of Iowa and has been associate director and professor at this University's famous interfaith School of Religion since 1942. He was the first man to receive a doctorate in the field of creative writing in religion from this School. World traveler, author and popular interpreter of intercultural relations, Dr. Bach has lived intimately with more than 40 different religious groups in seeking a common belief basic to all men.* Who Knows—and What *lists him as the foremost authority on contemporary religious movements and analyst of the American scene. His previous books include* They Have Found a Faith *(Bobbs-Merrill, 1946),* Report to Protestants *(Bobbs-Merrill, 1948),* Dream Gate *(Bobbs-Merrill, 1949),* Faith and My Friends *(Bobbs-Merrill, 1951),* Strange Altars *(Bobbs-Merrill, 1952), and* The Will to Believe *(Prentice-Hall, 1956).*

THE CIRCLE OF FAITH *(Hawthorn, 1957) was designed and printed by T. E. Devlin Company, Inc., East Paterson, New Jersey, and bound by Montauk Book Manufacturing Company, New York City. The body type is Linotype Caledonia, designed by W. A. Dwiggins, one of America's best-known typographers and designers.*

A HAWTHORN BOOK